STUDIES IN MARXISM, Vol. 9

The Philosophy
of Marxism:
An Exposition

■ JOHN SOMERVILLE

Professor Emeritus, City University of New York

MARXIST EDUCATIONAL PRESS
Minneapolis

For Susan Somerville
on her first day

This book is a reprint of the original 1967 edition.

Library of Congress Catalog Number 81-82196
ISBN 0-930656-17-2
ISBN 0-930656-18-0 pbk.

Printed in the United States of America
1981

MARXIST EDUCATIONAL PRESS
c/o Anthropology Department
University of Minnesota
215 Ford Hall, 224 Church St. S.E.
Minneapolis, Minnesota 55455

Publisher's Foreword to 1981 Printing

The need for reprinting John Somerville's *The Philosophy of Marxism: An Exposition* was first signaled by a University of Minnesota faculty team who have been teaching an introductory course on Marxism since 1975. The principal reading assignments for the first section of the course are selections from the original writings of Marx, Engels, and Lenin *(Reader in Marxist Philosophy*, ed. Howard Selsam and Harry Martel, New York: International Publishers, 1963). Most students are encountering the classics of Marxism for the first time, and when the course was first offered, many complained about the difficulty of the readings. It was then decided to begin with Somerville's *The Philosophy of Marxism: An Exposition*, after which the readings from the classics were assigned.

Student response was enthusiastic. Somerville had unlocked the door that gave access to the rich philosophical content in the writings of Marx, Engels, and Lenin. The reason for this was twofold. First, the classics of Marxism were not written as introductory texts. Somerville introduces the students to language, method, and subject matter previously strange to them and often initially forbidding. Second, Somerville's exposition of Marxist philosophy closely follows the spirit of the classics. He sees no necessity of "reinterpreting," "modernizing," selecting "only what is valid today," or otherwise introducing distortions of content so that the philosophy loses all connection with the revolutionary spirit of its founders. Moreover, Somerville raises questions that students usually ask and provides explanations in the context of the society in which they are living.

Both the close correspondence between the content of Somerville's exposition and the classics of Marxism, and the relevance of its form of presentation to U.S. readers, make the book an invaluable tool in the classroom. Its clarity and readibility make it suitable also for the general reader.

Since the original publication of *The Philosophy of Marxism: An Exposition*, there has been considerable discussion among Marxist scholars about the relationship between dialectical contradictions and formal-logical contradictions. A collection of recent articles can be found in the book *Dialectical Contradictions*, edited by Erwin Marquit, Philip Moran, and Willis H. Truitt, and published by Marxist Educational Press as Volume 10 in the present series *Studies in Marxism*. Discussions have also appeared from time to time in the journal *Soviet Studies in Philosophy*, which is edited by Professor Somerville and published in New York.

Professor Somerville is the author of the following books: *Methodology in Social Science, Soviet Philosophy: A Study of Theory and Practice, The Philosophy of Peace, The Way of Science, The Communist Trials and the American Tradition, Social and Political Philosophy* (with R. E. Santoni), *The Peace Revolution: Ethos and Social Process, The Crisis: The True Story About How the World Almost Ended* (play). Volumes of his selected essays have appeared in Russian and in Japanese. His most recent book is *Philosophy and Ethics in the Nuclear Age: For Human Survival* (in Japanese, 1980).

The original edition contained an appendix on debates among Marxists current in the sixties. The omission of this appendix is the only change introduced in the present printing.

MARXIST EDUCATIONAL PRESS
Minneapolis, Minnesota

Preface

It has been clear for some time now that it would be impossible to understand the world of the twentieth century without an understanding of Marx. His work, like that of Freud or Darwin, represents one of those tremendous forces which have made—and are still in process of making—our time different from other times.

The controversies surrounding Marxism are worldwide and unusually sharp. Indeed, they are not only *about* Marxism, but *within* Marxism. However, before one can judge these polemics, or take any intelligent part in them, one must first of all have a grasp of the basic ideas in question. The point may be put this way: we need to know the common core of doctrine that the great majority of Marxists accept, whatever differences may exist among them. It is the purpose of this book to try to make clear what that common core of doctrine is, when stated as a systematic philosophy in terms which include developments up to our day. The "Questions and Replies" that follow each chapter reflect the author's experience, over many years, in regard to specific points of difficulty, confusion, and misunderstanding that repeatedly arise among students and readers of Marxist works.

Whatever degree of clarity the author has been able to attain he owes in large part to a small family circle and a numerous student body; each in its own way afforded constant opportunities to undertake alternative explanations, the relative success and failure of which were made manifest. To these more or less captive audiences, already aware of the author's abiding affection, he wishes to express his deep gratitude.

J.S.

June, 1967

Contents

PART ONE

Overall Philosophic Principles

1.

The Nature of Reality:
Dialectical Materialism

Let us begin with the question: What sort of totality are we a part of? In human experience, this is not an avoidable question. It may be a matter for controversy whether we shall ever arrive at an answer that is satisfactory to everyone. But it is hardly controversial that everyone has felt the impact of the question, and would dearly like to have an answer. One might say that its impact at the level of intellectual consciousness is as inevitable—and as varied in form—as the impact of sex at the level of physiological consciousness.

In other words, every human being, at quite an early age, begins to ask himself and others: Who made this world? What was it made for? What was it made out of? How big is the whole thing? When did it begin? When will it end? What happens to people after they die? Without at this point going into its various causes, the fact is clear enough that even a child, not to speak of an adult, feels it impossible simply to accept without explanation the set of surroundings and activities in which he finds himself. If a child were to wake up some morning in an extremely large house he had never seen before, with all sorts of people doing all sorts of things, he would feel compelled to ask: What kind of house is this? Whose house is it? How did it get here? What is being done here? The world is like such a house; and the child raises just such questions about it. He feels the need to come to terms with the thing as a whole. He may eventually settle for negative terms, such as, "one can't find out," which is also a judgment, an answer; but in that case he will always wish there were a better one.

All this is true of children in a simple sense, and of adults in a more complex sense. Such questions about the world as a whole, the universe, the totality of which man is a part, become the basis of that branch of philosophy which is traditionally called metaphysics or ontology. It is obvious that these questions, as questions, are very real, and that the acceptance of different answers makes a great difference in the lives of people—in their attitudes, their feelings, their relationships, their expectations, the quality of their hopes and fears, the whole tone of their lives.

Still, there is great debate about the *meaning* of such questions in the intellectual, the purely cognitive sense. We are all aware that many forms of nonsense can have great emotional significance for people, can strongly affect their feelings and their lives in all sorts of ways. The acceptance of the reality of witches and demons not only could, but once did, and for rather a long time, make a very real difference, which on occasion became the difference between life and death. Treatises were written on witchcraft and demonology by respected teachers with influence and authority in the highest circles. The laws of the state and the church agreed on the point; each took pains to punish, not those who taught that people could be transformed into "witches," but the "witches." Clearly, the mere fact that one believes in and lives by something is not of itself sufficient evidence that that something has real, as distinct from fictional, existence; that, intellectually, it makes sense, as distinct from nonsense.

Having said this, we must also bear in mind that, if someone asks a question that someone else answers in a nonsensical way, the answer does not necessarily make the questioner guilty of nonsense. If the cattle in some village are unaccountably dying, and all the established authorities are looking for the practitioners of witchcraft who brought this calamity down upon the community, that does not necessarily make the question, "Why did the cattle die?" a nonsensical question. It all depends on what the given questioner means by it. If in his mind it is in fact equivalent to "Who are the guilty witches?" then it is indeed nonsense. But the questioner, of course, may not be limiting himself to such a construction.

The point we need to settle now is how Marxism construes these questions concerning the world in general, the totality—its composition, extent, duration, basic laws, its origin if any, end if any, purpose if any.

Marxism poses these questions about the totality only in a sense that permits an answer in terms of objective evidence—that is, evidence which goes back to observation, experiment, and logical analysis of the results of observation and experiment. Another way of saying the same thing is that Marxism seeks the answers to these questions about the totality by putting together—generalizing—the results of the various sciences. A negative way of putting the same point would be to say that Marxism rejects in principle, as illusory and fruitless, all mystical or supernaturalistic approaches.

Marxism classifies itself philosophically as materialism. One should note at once that, in using this term, its frame of emotional and valuational reference is not that of cynicism, bitterness, or depravity, but rather of confidence in the powers of human reason, as well as in the potentialities of nature and matter. The effort is clearly to get away from a faith or authority that claims to be above reason, from revelation, mystery, and miracle as ways of answering questions about the totality, and to stick to the methods of science.

This approach means, for one thing, that Marxist materialism holds no unalterable conception of matter. Its attitude is that it is willing to follow specific sciences in whatever further discoveries about matter are possible, and that many more are certainly to be expected. Thus Marxists are not exactly saying, "We hold that reality is matter, and that matter is limited to such and such properties." Rather, they are saying, "By reality we mean that which is objectively confirmable by evidence and reason. Matter is the general name given to the basic content of that existence which is confirmable by evidence and reason. The name does not settle its characteristics and properties. These can be settled only by further and further investigations, which may indeed be endless. But they must be scientific investigations, and the conclusions must be rationally demonstrable." Thus it would be an oversimplification of the meaning of materialism, as Marxism sees it, to say that its basic proposition is that nothing exists except matter. It is rather that nothing exists except matter and its functions, properties, and powers of development.

To say simply, "Reality is matter," may seem to suggest an intention to deny full reality to anything that is not directly physical or material, such as ideas and ideals. Marxism does not have this intention. It fully recognizes the real existence of ideas, ideals, moral and esthetic values, intellectual abstractions, and the like. What it insists upon is that the objective evidence shows all such levels and forms of reality to be genetically connected with, to grow out of, basic forms of matter; that there is no evidence that they grow out of anything else, and no rational need to assume that they grow out of anything else. Matter itself, in its simplest forms, is active, dynamic, functional; it is never really passive or inert. The evidence shows that it is capable of change, development, evolution. These facts are sufficient to account rationally for the genesis of differentiated structures, higher levels, complex functions.

Thus Marxism would reject the Platonic conception that pure abstract ideas are the basic reality, the primary and eternal reality, of which tangible and material things are merely passing shadows, imperfect and transitory copies. If such pure ideas had primary existence, how would they generate transitory material copies? Where is the explanation of such a process or any evidence that it takes place? The Marxist points out that if we begin with active matter, which in fact is universally evident and demonstrably characterized by capability of change and development, we can rationally account for the emergence of complex forms, for the evolution of one form out of another, of the organic out of the inorganic, for the appearance of animals with nervous systems, memory, and learning capacity. Then we can account for the formation of ideas in terms of the traceable functioning of a physiological nervous system and an observable brain structure.

Platonic idealism, like Cartesian rationalism, puts the

cart before the horse. As Plato argued for the primacy of ideas, so Descartes did for the primacy of the thinking process, of mind. Both neglected the evidence (some of which was available to them, but most of which has been brought forth since) that ideas and thought processes are not primary, but are the results of the functioning of physiological and neurological organs and powers, ultimately traceable to their bodily sources. The concept of an immaterial mind, not dependent in any way on body or matter—the premise and starting point of Cartesian rationalism—has receded with the progress of science. To Plato's contention that the senses lead us astray, that we would be better off without the body, with pure mind in contact with pure ideas, the Marxist replies: Without the senses and the body, there would not be pure mind and pure ideas. There would be no mind and no ideas.

But then the question immediately arises: Granted that we can account for the rise of the simplest forms of living matter by evolution (further evolution) of the most complex forms of inorganic matter, and for the rise of nervous systems and brain structures in the same way, how can we account for matter itself, in its simplest forms? The Marxist's answer to this question is in no way original. Most materialist philosophy (which has had a long history, going back to pre-Socratic "physicalism" and earlier traditions) gives essentially the same answer: As there never could have been just nothing, the most rational conclusion we can come to is that matter, in some form, was always existent.

Why is this conclusion regarded as the most rational? First, because if we wish to use reason, we cannot claim or assume that we can get something from nothing. We obviously do have something now—a totality of some kind. Even the solipsist, who is sure only of himself or his own consciousness, says that there is something, i.e., himself. If the something we have now did not come from nothing, it must have come from something else. As the same applies to this something else, the only rational conclusion is that existence in its totality must be an eternal, interconnected system, which had no absolute starting point, since such a starting point would mean getting something from nothing.

If existence goes through processes of change and evolution, as it obviously does, it is clear that the same forms of existence that we now see need not always have existed. Yet at any particular time something must have existed. By the same reasoning, we reach the conclusion that there always will be something. That is, just as we cannot get something from nothing, so also we cannot get nothing from something, though it may sometimes seem that we do. When we speak of destroying something, it cannot be in an absolute sense, into nothingness. What we do is break up the form, arrangement, structure; another form, arrangement, structure is thereby produced. This whole situation has been summed up in the principle of conservation of matter or energy; none can be either created or destroyed, in the absolute sense.

This line of reasoning is often confronted with the objections of those who claim they are unable to imagine, to conceive rationally, anything without a beginning. The Marxist philosopher answers as many other philosophers do: This is because these people have in mind only particular, finite things. While their conclusion is perfectly true for each particular and finite thing, they are failing to observe that, precisely because it is true that each particular thing must have a beginning from something else, the total *series* of particular things could not have a beginning, for if the series as a whole had a beginning, the first unit would not have come from something else.

In other words, a series, each unit of which must come from a preceding unit, must be an infinite series, without a starting point. In no other way could the condition be fulfilled of each unit coming from a preceding unit. Actually, everyone is quite familiar with such a series, for example, in arithmetic. Anyone who has heard of negative numbers understands that minus three is less than minus two, so that there is no "lowest number" in the series of numbers, just as there is no "highest number." The series is obviously beginningless or endless in either direction. Yet that fact does not make the series either inconceivable or unusable. The most that can be said is that the whole series is *physically* unimaginable, in the sense of a single perceptual image taking it all in at once. But such an image is not logically necessary. Nor is it necessary for the concept of the totality of existence.

It is significant to notice that many schools of thought opposed to materialism also feel the logical need to maintain that something must have existed eternally. But the materialist holds that, for one reason or another, they do not carry through the logic of their positions consistently. Various theological philosophies, for example, hold that God is the eternal guarantor of existence, the something that always was and always will be. But this God is conceived of as an incomprehensible, purely spiritual Being, who created the tangible, understandable universe out of nothing in a way human reason could never grasp. The materialist maintains that such assumptions needlessly abandon logic. If logic tells us that whatever was earlier must have given rise to whatever came later, how are we helped by construing the earlier phase as supernatural and incomprehensible—especially when we have sciences, constantly improving, that explain rationally how things are brought into existence by other things?

In this regard, the materialist finds especially vulnerable the famous "Argument from Design," which points out that so complex a thing as the entire natural universe could not have come into existence accidentally. Logically, so the argument goes, we must assume a supernatural Designer capable of creating all that complexity. But then, by the same logic, we would have to assume a super-supernatural Designer to account for the supernatural Designer, a super-super-supernatural Designer to account for the super-supernatural Designer, and so on. What we here are really saying (again) is that reason tells us there is a sequence of existences, that later existences must have come from earlier ones, and thus existence must always have existed. The materialist concludes that, if there is no beginning, there is no need for a Beginner.

We have already, in speaking of Plato, noted the kind of criticism that the materialist directs against idealism. That is, to say that ideas are primary and eternal makes it impossible to account rationally for matter. We have no evidence to explain how ideas could generate tangible things; but we do have adequate evidence, in physics, chemistry, and biology, to explain how tangible things come to generate ideas. In this connection, the materialist emphasizes the close relation that exists between idealism and supernatural theology, a relation that is reflected also in the remark by Bertrand Russell (himself no materialist) that "Christianity is the poor man's Platonism." That is, pure mind, or pure idea, which is supposed to give rise, inexplicably, to material things, becomes personified in the conception of God the Father, who, by an act of omnipotent will, miraculously creates the universe out of nothing.

We have so far dealt with the Marxist view of the totality of existence in regard to its possible origin, duration, extent, and basic composition. What about purpose? The answer to this question might be deduced from what has been said concerning the other issues. The purpose of anything is by definition a relationship to something further. Since there can be nothing *beyond* the totality of existence, the totality as a totality can no more have a purpose than it can have an origin. But there can be all sorts of purposes *within* the totality—purposes of parts in relation to other parts. A person, an institution, a state, an object—each of these can have a purpose, because there is something else for each of them to relate to.

This line of thought calls forth in some the objection that it presents a kind of negative or empty picture of the totality, a picture that deprives the human being of something precious. To the Marxist, this objection represents a feeling more than a logical argument, a feeling which is relative to the way people are brought up and taught. If they are conditioned from an early age to believe in the existence of certain things, to which they then become attached, but which do not accord with facts that later emerge, they will feel that to recognize such facts, and their implications, would be to take something away from themselves.

In any case, the Marxist denies that his materialist conception of the universe is a negative or empty one. He feels it is a conception that actually gives man a much greater role, much more dignity and stature than the theological or idealistic conception gives him. Man is not the creature of an omnipotent Creator, whose ways he is unable to understand, but whose commands he must nevertheless obey. Man is a being who can gain more and more objective knowledge of the totality of which he is a part, of the forces that have produced him; since objective knowledge is also power, he can gain by his knowledge more and more power in relation to those forces. All this puts man in a closer, more responsible, and more creative position in relation to the totality of which he is a part. It makes him to a greater extent the architect and master of his own fate. In an infinite, eternal universe, operating in terms of natural sequences and forces, he has the greatest scope for his powers, the greatest range for his efforts, and the greatest potential of interest, adventure, and emotional richness for his life.

In such a universe can there be any place for ideals, moral values, moral obligation? The Marxist philosopher points out that such questions as these arise largely because people have grown so accustomed to associating moral obligations and values with the commands of an all-powerful God who threatens punishment for disobedience, that they assume moral values and obligations to be capable of having no other source; or, if they do have another source, then they must, for that reason alone, be less than genuine, not really binding. Dostoevsky, through a number of his characters, expressed this view in the formulation: If there is no God, everything is possible. There would be no binding standards.

The materialist, by contrast, takes the view that the ultimate source of values, obligations, and ideals is man's needs and man's ability to create. He further holds that this fact does not degrade values and obligations, but rather elevates man. The appeal to follow moral standards then becomes an appeal to man's own self-respect, to his own intelligence and creativity. One might call this "self-government" in the sphere not only of politics, but of morality in life as a whole. In the supernatural approach to morals, Marxism detects a fundamental attitude of paternalism or autocracy rather than of self-government.

Must "ideals" be thought of as if they stood, inherently and by definition, in *opposition* to matter and body? The materialist rejects the view that matter, body, physical, and the like are "dirty words." That is too superficial a view; among those who profess to hold it, the result is often hypocrisy. To the materialist, ideals and values are concepts that point to the best uses of, the most fruitful ways of dealing with, that which enters man's life. Matter is not in principle regrettable; it is a source of value.

Perhaps every world view is an attitude, as well as a doctrine. As an attitude toward the totality, materialism is compounded of at least three elements: (*a*) a desire to *understand*, rather than just to accept, adjust to, have faith in, or esthetically feel, the totality; (*b*) the premise that the best way to gain *responsible* understanding (and thus to improve our practice in relation to the parts we deal with) is to use the methods of science; and

(c) the conclusion that science does not mix with supernaturalism, revelation, or mysticism. This attitude does not mean that acceptance, adjustment, faith, or esthetic feeling are to be ruled out of life, but rather that they are not to be taken as the basis, the determining factor, of a world view. The aim of a world view is to gain truth which benefits man; and truth, first and foremost, must be objective—which means scientific. Agnosticism is ruled out as a hopeless attempt to avoid an unavoidable problem, while eclecticism is ruled out as an unprincipled attempt to profess allegiance to both sides of a contest.

Let us try to illustrate some aspects of this basic attitude which characterizes materialism. Take, for example, such a phenomenon as love. The materialist's attitude is not that it should be belittled or discouraged as an activity, emotion, or feeling, unless, of course, it is being pursued in some destructive way. Neither is his attitude the cynical one that "love does not exist," or that it is not necessary to take seriously the question of standards, values, and ideals in relation to it. His attitude is that love is obviously a very important part of life, but that its importance is as an emotional fact, not as an explanation. More explanation does not mean less love; neither does more love mean less explanation. Man needs more of both.

To explain any fact, to understand its place in life, we must employ reason. Reason is not a substitute for feeling; it is the only means of explaining feeling. Such explanation not only need not destroy or diminish the feeling involved; on the contrary, it is clearly capable of contributing positively to it. Increasing knowledge of the facts of love, through physiology, psychology, and sociology, helps to avert unhappiness and tragedy, and to bring many factors under control, so that love can be more successfully consummated as a reality in people's lives.

The same thing holds true of man's entire emotional life, including his esthetic appreciation and artistic creativity, very important aspects of which are matters of emotion and feeling. Their value and significance as experiences, as phases of life, is one thing. The explanation of them—in terms of their basis, causes, and effects, their operation and impact—is quite another thing. The two categories are related, but they must not be confused.

It is interesting to note that, in this attitude, the materialist is at one with many classic thinkers, especially of the ancient Greek world, whom we do not usually think of as having anything in common with materialism. The approach of Aristotle, for instance, places human reason in the center of the stage, and leaves no room for supernaturalism, either in ontology or in morals. Not only is man capable of genuine understanding, but everything can be understood. It is only a question of time and discipline. The same attitude is found in Democritus, Epicurus, Lucretius, Leucippus, Empedocles and many others, and in such modern thinkers as Bacon, Hobbes, Spinoza, and Mill.

Another way of putting this point is in terms of the role of faith as distinct from the role of reason. For example, a traditional and still widely influential theological position is that reason should be used for all questions and problems for which it is adequate, but that there are many questions—including some of the most important that man must ask—for which reason is not adequate. The truth about such questions, according to this view, is attainable only through something higher than reason—namely, faith. The truth that is yielded by this faith is usually considered to be revealed to man in certain sacred scriptures, or implanted in him in the form of intuitive feelings. Such a view is reflected in Pascal's claim that "The heart has its reasons, which reason does not understand," in Kant's concept of the supernaturally implanted categorical imperative, which allegedly gives us the basis of morality, and in the interpretation of conscience as a mysterious spiritual force.

The materialist attitude is that there is nothing that can properly be called truth, over and above that which is a product of logical analysis working upon the data that are supplied by the senses through careful observation and experiment. People do have strong intuitions, deep and powerful feelings about all sorts of things, including moral judgments. But there is no need to assume that these feelings are mystical or supernaturally derived, in the sense of being scientifically inexplicable. They can be rationally traced to their sources and their causes in man's psychological and social life. But the strength or depth with which one feels that something is *true* is, unfortunately, no necessary index of its actual truth. Its truth can be established only by rational methods and objective evidence.

If faith is defined broadly enough to include any sense of trust in the future reliability of something, its future success in operation and outcome, then it would be fair to say that the materialist has faith in man and in the power of his reason. But he would argue that this is an informed rather than an arbitrary faith, and has its basis in confirmable appraisal of past experience. In other words, there is a significant difference between a mystical faith and a rational faith.

There is also a significant difference between the argument of a St. Thomas Aquinas, who holds there is a truth higher than that yielded by reason (not contradictory to reason, but supplementary to it), which truth we should accept as an explanation, and the position of philosophers who, like Plato, remain committed in principle exclusively to reason, yet make what the materialist regards as cardinal errors, judged by rational criteria.

In any case, the materialist holds that the term "truth" should be reserved only for that which is demonstrable by objectively rational methods, and that the truth in that sense is man's best guide and explanation. Truth is regarded as having both an absolute and a relative dimension—absolute in the sense that at any given time there exists a definite and objective reality, a state of affairs which in principle could be fully known and exactly stated, yet relative in the sense that at any given time the truth we possess in the form of knowledge about that reality is not complete.

Practically all we have said so far represents aspects of the world view or ontology that Marxism inherited from preceding materialist philosophy. Before examining what it added to its inheritance, let us emphasize the significance of the historical setting. One must remember that philosophy is a very old term, which, until quite recently (up to the eighteenth century) was employed as a name for knowledge in its entirety. There was no distinction in principle between science and philosophy; the terms were used synonymously. In other words, what we now call the sciences, whether physical or social, were regarded as parts of philosophy; those who cultivated them were called philosophers. If the individual scholar was interested mainly in questions concerning the physical world or the phenomena of organic nature, he was called a natural philosopher; if he dealt with social questions, he was called a civil philosopher; if his specialty was theology, he was a divine philosopher, and so on.

We sometimes forget that many great figures whose work we now think of as science, and whom we therefore classify as scientists, themselves thought of their work as philosophy, and referred to themselves as philosophers. Isaac Newton, for example, published his great work under the title, *Mathematical Principles of Natural Philosophy*. Even as late as the beginning of the nineteenth century in England, John Dalton, who is known as the father of the modern concept of the atom, entitled the results of his investigations *New Principles of Chemical Philosophy*. To none of the thinkers of the Renaissance, among whom we identify the pioneers and founders of what we call modern physical or natural science, did the word science (or *scientia* in the Latin which they mainly used) have any special meaning, as distinct from philosophy or knowledge in general.

We find a like situation if we look at the history of the social or behavioral sciences. The father of sociology, Auguste Comte, who coined the term, and was the first to present a large-scale systematic treatise dealing with the field specifically as a science, entitled his work *Cours de philosophie positive* less than a century and a half ago. In fact, Comte is still approached as much in his capacity of "philosopher" as in that of "sociologist." We see the same situation in the case of an even more recent figure such as William James, who is equally regarded as philosopher and as psychologist.

All this is neither a matter of arbitrary terminology nor simply of exceptional versatility. It is an indication of a profoundly significant historical fact: all the special sciences are outgrowths of philosophy, which has been like a tree, giving rise to branches as it develops. In other words, philosophy creates sciences. Put differently, what we have come to call scientific knowledge is one kind of philosophy, the product of one kind of method and approach.

This method or approach is, of course, that which relies on sense data, observation, experiment, and logical analysis. It necessarily had to reject any authority or tradition that claimed to possess "revealed" truth from a supernatural source, if such truth stood in contradiction to what was found by the method of natural reason. It is perhaps not necessary to emphasize that what we are here describing represents a gigantic social conflict: To challenge the claims of revelation and of supernatural authority was to challenge the existing social system at its foundations.

All through the Middle Ages and the Renaissance, the church assumed the responsibility and had the power to carry on and control education at all levels, and to do likewise with intellectual life generally. Responsibility and control (in Europe) were of course conceived and enforced in relation to the doctrines of the Christian religion, and therefore rested upon supernatural authority and revelation. The very powers of the state, the right of the king to rule in a certain way, the validity of civil and criminal law, were likewise considered to be based upon the revealed truths of supernatural religion. To challenge supernaturalistic revelation as a warrant of truth, in relation to any questions on which it had taken a public stand, was therefore a most grave and dangerous matter.

Each instance of a challenge to what was taken to be revealed truth, or truth certified by established authority, became a pitched battle, in which the church-state combination had an immense superiority of weapons, including the power to imprison and put to death. Efforts to apply to the basic questions of astronomy and physics the methods we now call scientific, and to argue for acceptance of the results of such methods, required such a high degree of courage, in addition to extraordinary intellectual gifts, that undoubtedly most of those who might have made important contributions were inhibited even from trying. In the circumstances, some great thinkers—including Copernicus and Spinoza—adopted the expedient of concealing their major work until the end of their lives, hoping for posthumous publication, which could, of course, itself be delayed or defeated. Many men of the stature of Galileo, Bruno, Campanella, and Telesio were deprived of teaching posts, imprisoned, or put to death, because they were found guilty of contradicting revealed "truth" and of opposing sacred authorities.

Most of these courageous and talented thinkers fought their battle over some particular problem, such as the nature of motion, or in some particular field, such as the astronomy of the planetary system. Few of them tried to argue for the application of the method they were using to all matters in which truth was claimed. Even had they wished to do so, this might well have seemed too much to attempt, where to try so little was so dangerous. Materialism is the philosophic name for the doctrine and attitude that this general attempt should be made, and will be successful, in all fields.

Let us now examine what Marxism added to this tradition of materialist philosophy. In a general sense, of course, all the traditional materialist approaches and attitudes were expressed and implemented by Marx and Engels in terms of new situations, new problems, new content. But, in addition to this general reworking, there are certain specific doctrines—qualitatively new in relation to the materialist tradition—that Marx and Engels incorporated into it, with results which have exercised a tremendous influence.

The briefest way of expressing what they did is to say that they made materialism dialectical, whereas it had been predominantly mechanistic. What was involved in this? The effort of materialism had always been to "take nature without reservations," as Engels once put it— that is, to explain the totality in terms of the natural, humanly discoverable, and humanly understandable operation of causes, effects, and laws, without assuming anything mystical, or in principle incomprehensible, above it or behind it. Up to the time of Marx and Engels (who were contemporaries of Darwin) this approach had produced a general picture of the world that could be expressed as the universal operation of cause-effect and of law within a set of basic patterns that were static and eternal. In other words, the most basic aspects of reality were regarded as unchanging. History was not seen as central or primary in relation to matter.

Of course, change and motion were recognized, but they were considered to be on the surface rather than of the essence, to be relative to a framework that was fixed and fundamental. Heavenly bodies moved, but in constant orbits. Individual animals were born, grew, and died, but the animal species were fixed. Different objects were formed by different combinations of atoms, but the atoms themselves were impenetrable and impervious to change. Qualitative changes came about through the interaction of chemical elements, but the elements themselves were immutable. This was a rational universe, in the sense that things were accounted for in terms of the action of mechanisms; nevertheless, these mechanisms, in their basic aspects, and in the laws of their action, did not have any history. Qualitative changes were brought about, but that which brought them about did not undergo qualitative, but only quantitative, changes. Things died out and were replaced; but they did not evolve, nor did they grow into new types. In Marxist literature, this conception of the universe or totality is called "metaphysical," as well as "mechanistic" materialism because the term "metaphysics" has been traditionally identified with doctrines of an eternally changeless reality.

Marx and Engels held that the progress of science made it more and more clear that this view of the universe was oversimplified. It left out a dimension that was absolutely fundamental; or, at best, it relegated this utterly primary aspect of reality, an aspect that pervaded its very foundations, to a place of secondary, merely relative significance. We are referring, of course, to the dimension of change—not simply in the restricted, mechanical sense of quantitative changes, but in the evolutionary sense of pervasive, qualitative change at the roots.

This is clearly a conception of tremendous import—

one that was, in its essence, by no means original with Marx and Engels. (What was original with them was its elaboration within the framework of modern material- ism, at the level of modern science.) Since everything is in motion, and capable of going through a process of development involving qualitative changes, it follows that nothing is absolutely static. Insofar as we know the universe—that is, in accordance with all the evidence we possess—it is a *process* as much as a *thing*. Put differ- ently, it is a thing that is constantly in process, or a process which manifests itself in the form of a series of things. The evidence shows that what seems changeless is slowly changing; what seems stationary is only so rela- tive to a point of observation that is itself moving. Our totality is, through and through, a dynamic one.

The word "dialectical" is used to express this sort of continuous change, which is thorough and proceeds from one extreme to another. In philosophy, "dialecti- cal" is an ancient term, employed to express the course of an argument that moves from one view to its oppo- site, from the upholding of an idea to the upholding of its denial through the establishing of a contradictory idea, to the upholding of a denial of that denial, and so on.

It is important to recognize that the contention of Marx and Engels that reality is dialectical is meant to apply to every level and aspect of reality, not only to the directly physical level dealt with by such sciences as as- tronomy, physics, chemistry, and biology. This pervasive- ness and thoroughness of change and evolution is seen equally at the social level, the moral level, the esthetic level, and the intellectual level. We have grown accus- tomed to the fact that the cosmos is a scene of universal motion and change, that atoms are penetrable, elements mutable, and species evolvable. We must be prepared, says the dialectical materialist, to reorient ourselves in the same sense to the content and problems of such fields as sociology, psychology, esthetics, and logic.

This aspect of the Marxist's world view also manifests itself as an attitude—one that might be called, in his terms, the dialectical attitude. It comprises three factors: (*a*) an acceptance of basic qualitative changes as the natural results of processes that have pervaded the past history of the totality; (*b*) an expectation that such processes will continue into the future; and (*c*) a desire to adjust both theory and practice to these processes.

The issue here involved, and the difference that it makes, can be seen and felt in the historical impact of such significant developments as Copernican astronomy and Darwinian biology. After Copernicus had completed his work, and its validity had become clear, man was forced to alter, in certain profound respects, his whole attitude toward his earthly world, an alteration that could not help bringing about significant changes in his attitude toward what he had been taught concerning the heavenly world. These changes of attitude in turn threatened the foundations of power exercised by the church and the state. When the earth was regarded as the unmoving center of the universe, not only were intellectual teachings worked out in accordance with this presumption; a whole psychological and emotional set went along with them, and was threatened when they were threatened. If one can imagine being suddenly told that the house in which he has lived since childhood, and which he has come to regard as a very symbol of what is stable and securely rooted, is really on wheels, moving into some unknown region, he might then feel, to a very slight degree, the kind of difference the Copernican theory made.

The difference between moving and not moving, between changing and not changing, is a very profound one; it is almost as great as the difference between life and death. In some ways it could even be greater, so far as adjustment to it is concerned. If the life in question is one whose course we are familiar with, as in the case of a puppy we thought was dead, yet which turns out to be alive, we can adjust to this reversal with relative ease. But if the motion or change we are suddenly made aware of is carrying us in an unknown direction, into regions of which no one has had previous experience, adjustment to the situation is not so easy. Psychologically and emotionally, there is first of all a tremendous resistance to accepting the new fact, a very strong willingness not only to deny it, but to treat even the most rational demonstrations of its validity as sins and crimes, worthy of opprobrium and severe punishment, and to suppress the new view. These are, of course, recognizable fear reactions—in this case, fear of the unknown, and of loss of accustomed power.

We have witnessed more recently the same pattern of events in connection with the work of Darwin. The idea, even when supported by adequate evidence, that species themselves, and not only the individual beings within them, were capable of change and development, and that the species man had thus evolved from lower and simpler species, could not be accepted without a tremendous struggle. Even as late as 1925 in the United States, a teacher of biology could be tried (and found guilty) of violating a state law by teaching Darwinian evolution.

Marxist philosophy makes two basic points in relation to these problems. First, it would have been better had the world view of the people involved recognized the pervasiveness of change and development, so that they could have made allowances for it. Second, it is better now to recognize that this pervasiveness is not restricted to the subject matter of such fields as astronomy and biology, but must be expected in all subject matter. The world view, the attitude of man to the totality, must be one that is prepared for basic changes all along the line.

For example, in respect to man's social life, the issue presents itself first of all as a question of one's underlying attitude toward the very possibility of changes in the basic institutions, laws, and patterns of power that make up human society. Is it the operative attitude that social institutions and patterns can remain basically the same in the future, with changes restricted to details and to personnel? This issue must be faced first, apart from the subsequent issue of what possible basic changes are desirable or inevitable.

Another way of putting this primary issue is to ask whether or not human society is in process of evolution at all, whether there is any dialectic, materialist or otherwise, pervading it. Is the present condition of human society, in terms of the nature of its institutions, power patterns, and laws, a stage or phase of a general process? If it is, we should obviously be deeply concerned to gain knowledge about this process. That would be a precondition of successful development, perhaps even of survival.

Broadly speaking, one may point to three different attitudes in relation to the possibility of social evolution, as distinct from small-scale changes. One attitude is to deny that there is any such evolution. A second is that it is possible, but would make no difference to us; that is, there would be nothing in particular for us to do, since it would come about, anyway. The third is that there is in fact such an evolution, and that there is something valuable and important for us to do about it.

This third attitude is that of the Marxist. What evidence does he adduce to support it? He points first of all to the past. Society has already gone through stages of development that are tremendously different from one another in terms of institutions, power patterns, and basic laws. These changes represent qualitative transitions. The transitions from prehuman to cave man, from primitive communal groupings to a complex slave society, from slave society to feudalism, from feudalism to modern industrial society—these are not simply quantitative changes, larger amounts or aggregates of the same basic forms, institutions, and laws. They involve the emergence of qualitative differences, of radically new patterns and institutions. The Marxist attitude, in this regard shared by a number of other schools of thought, is that this social evolution can be studied and understood. With greater understanding will come greater power to predict, to gain control of what is controllable, and to make fruitful adjustments to what is not. In varying degrees this conception was developed before Marx by such thinkers as Hegel, St. Simon, and Comte, and later by many others, such as John Stuart Mill, Herbert Spencer, and John Dewey.

The Marxist sees the same dynamic, evolutionary patterns at the level of moral and esthetic values, and at the intellectual level of concepts and ideas. It is important to note here something that will be brought out more fully in the following chapter. That is, the processes of motion and change, development and evolution which are found at every level of existence, operate not only between things, by impact of one thing upon another, or as an external force, impinging upon the properties of a thing from some outside source, but within things, as an integral property of the most basic content of things. In other words, motion is an inalienable property of matter, and of all that matter produces. There is no matter without the motion and development proper to its level of existence.

Here again one sees the difference between the picture of the world drawn by mechanistic materialism and that drawn by materialism which is dialectical. In the former, the role attributed to motion has sometimes been expresssed by saying it presented a "billiard ball" conception of the universe. That is, the atoms composing all things were like billiard balls, each of which is motionless until pushed by another. The contrasting dialectical conception is expressed by saying that motion is, in the last analysis, self-motion. That is, it is a built-in property of matter, a necessary form of existence of matter in all its ramifications. If one were somehow able to imagine that one could touch successively each part or aspect of the totality, including feelings, values, and ideas, to the innermost reaches of reality, one would find everything stirring and growing, in every iota of its being.

As we have seen, the problem of ontology, in some ways the broadest and most basic part of philosophy, has often been epitomized in the question, "What is reality?" If we put this question to the dialectical materialist for a brief answer or summation, he will first have to point out the sense in which he construes the question. The necessity for this procedure arises from the fact that this question is sometimes asked with the implication, frequently met with in "classical" philosophy, that what is presented to us in ordinary experience is not reality, but only "appearance," behind which there is a "reality" that is incapable of being explained in terms of human experience. Such was Plato's doctrine of reality as a system of pure ideas, existing independently of material things and of human experience. These latter, as he saw it, constitute only appearance, and yield only opinion, as distinct from true knowledge. Such also was Kant's doctrine of "Things-in-Themselves," true knowledge of which could never be gained by human reason, as distinct from things as they appear to human experience and scientific reasoning.

This approach, which is called "dualism" because it makes the claim that the philosopher, in seeking to know reality, must deal with two *incommensurable* realms, is associated in philosophical literature with systems traditionally described as "metaphysical." In this fact we may note another reason why the Marxist rejects the term "metaphysics" as a proper designation of his world view or ontology, which, by contrast, is profoundly monistic. That is, as we have seen, the Marxist insists that there is no evidence of a realm unknowable by experience and human reason, and that there is no rational need to assume the existence of any such realm. To him, a valid ontology must be exclusively composed of those most general truths about existence that can be gained from human experience and human reason.

Understanding that the Marxist takes the question "What is reality?" in that sense, his answer to it might be summed up briefly as follows: Reality is all that is within us and outside of us, as apprehended through the processes of natural experience and comprehended through the methods of human reason and science. Reason tells us that this reality must be infinite and eternal, thus could have neither a "first cause" nor a single, overall "purpose." The various sciences tell us, on the basis of investigations pursued at every level, that this reality is pervasively characterized by motion, change, development, and evolution. It is obviously impossible for us to *describe* reality completely. But it is possible to define the conditions and methods in terms of which the process of description is carried further and further; and it is possible to state the confirmable results that have been attained so far. These are matters to which we shall return in the following chapter.

If this is the nature of the totality of which man is a part, what could be the "meaning" of his life? Again, the answer to the question depends on what is intended by its language. If one is seeking mystical (logically inexplicable) meanings from "higher" (supernatural) sources, the materialist—dialectical or other—will say bluntly, as we have seen, that it is impossible rationally to believe in any such meanings, since we have no rationally convincing evidence that they exist.

However, in a humanly understandable sense, man gives meaning to his own life by creating his goals and ideals. Of course, he does not create these out of nothing, but in relation, first, to the kind of creature he is, the kind of needs he has, and second, in relation to the given conditions that he faces in the particular surrounding environment. While man did not create the natural forces that produced him, and the total environment surrounding him, it is none the less true that within this framework he is a tremendous creator. He can make plans, and fulfill them. If the materialist says that nature creates life, and man creates values, he does not mean this in a dualistic or mystical sense, for he holds that these values are created on the basis of the conditions of life, and that life is created on the basis of the conditions of what we call matter.

QUESTIONS and REPLIES

1. *Materialism maintains that as a philosophy it bases itself upon science. Yet is it not possible to be a good scientist without being a materialist in one's philosophy?*

Only at the risk of inconsistency, and possibly of preventing oneself from becoming a still better scientist. Contemporary materialists recognize that a great many people who have made outstanding contributions to science were not materialists in their consciously-held philosophical outlook, taken as a whole. However, it is argued that these people were practising materialists in regard to the scientific work they did, in the sense that they relied exclusively upon human reason, without invoking supernatural faith or authority; that they restricted themselves to objective evidence, as based on observation, experiment, and the balance of probability, and refused to accept conclusions that went beyond these limits, or did not meet these standards. The fact that they did not carry the same approach further into their world view cannot be used legitimately as an argument against that approach. It simply leaves open the question of world view as a whole.

2. *Materialism relies on science. Yet has not science shown that energy has as good a claim as matter to be called the basis of all things?*

Contemporary Marxist materialists point out that their school of thought has always recognized that the characteristics and properties of matter could never be pinned down once and for all, in some doctrine that could claim to be fixed and final. Contemporary science has shown that what was previously called matter and what was previously called energy are convertible into each other. This discovery in no way disappoints the materialist; first, because it is based on the same methods—that is, further application of the same methods—of observation, experimentation, and logical analysis that brought into being the earlier and simpler concept of matter, which was relative to the knowledge then possessed; second, because the materialist has never denied the reality of energy, or denied that there was a connection between it and what was previously called matter. He insisted, in fact, that there was such a connection, but he never took a dogmatic stand that the connection had to be one that excluded mutual convertibility.

The discovery of this connection does not mean that matter has "disappeared," any more than it means energy has disappeared. When it was first discovered that the weasel and the ermine are not two different animals, but the same animal with different fur color at different seasons of the year, it would have been stretching the point to say that either the ermine or the weasel had "disappeared." Every good naturalist who had not previously thought that there was such a close connection as that between the "two" animals was presumably none the less glad to learn that this was so; on the other hand, it is difficult to see how the discovery could provide any lasting comfort to a good supernaturalist, who all along had been holding that neither the ermine nor the weasel, as naturalistically observed, contained the basic reality which we must recognize, and that this basic reality was in general not reachable naturalistically.

3. In spite of the Marxist's claim that he has rejected metaphysics, is not materialism itself, as an ontology or world view, a form of metaphysics?

What the Marxist materialist objects to in "metaphysics" is not the effort to seek for the most basic and general traits of existence or reality. He objects to certain methods and conclusions that have characterized many systems of thought traditionally called "metaphysical," their mystical, idealistic, nonscientific, and non-historical qualities. Therefore the term "metaphysics" is avoided in favor of the term "ontology" or world view.

4. Does materialism assert that it has disproved the existence of God? In spite of all that science has explained about the workings of the natural world, is it not still possible that there does exist a supernatural world, which cannot be understood by man's mind, yet which he can have faith in?

Logically speaking, it is not necessary to *disprove* the

existence of God. It is necessary only to show that the evidence offered in support of the existence of a supernatural deity does not in fact *prove* any such existence. When we are dealing with the question of the alleged existence of something, logical method does not require, or even permit, that its existence be taken as fact until it is disproved. It is rather the other way around: There is no need, or warrant, to believe in its existence until that existence has been proved. The materalist argues that it has never been possible to prove the existence of a supernatural deity by any appeal to facts, evidence, and reason—that is, by way of appeal to logic—and proof is, of course, a matter of logic. Any appeal to logic is necessarily based on our natural knowledge of the natural order, and must be comprehensible to the human mind. Belief in the supernatural is an act of faith, not a mandate of logic. If the universe had no beginning, then it has no logical need of a supernatural creator who made it out of nothing. If reason tells us that there is a *natural* order of existence, which is infinite (without beginning or end) and eternal, what rational need is there to postulate a *supernatural* existence that is also infinite and eternal?

The Marxist feels that "faith" in such supernatural concepts and entities is misplaced, that the emotional comfort it may bring is purchased at too high a price. This faith largely amounts to resigning oneself to whatever happens, in the hope that there is some good reason for it, even though no one knows what it is, and that all will be made right in some future life, even though no one knows how that will be done, or has any objective evidence that there is such a life. The materialist holds that faith should be placed in the development of man's own powers to understand and control his natural environment, since this kind of faith has a rational basis that is confirmed by past experience.

5. If science is the basis of the materialist world view maintained by Marxism, why speak of philosophy at all? Is philosophy really needed?

Philosophy in a certain traditional sense—the sense associated especially with the term "metaphysics"—is not needed. Put differently, a certain kind of philosophy is not needed—the kind that claims to have some way of gaining truth about the world and man that is not dependent upon the methods of science, and yet yields far more certainty than these methods. This kind of philosophy believes in a truth that is independent of sense perception and of the tangible, material world. The claims of such a philosophy are not vindicated in practice. It has no objective standard by which to determine the validity of its claims; and its doctrines add nothing to human power—the power to predict, and to control.

While that kind of philosophy, according to the Marxist, is not needed, there is a vital need for philosophy as a synthesis and generalization of the work that has been done and is being done in the separate sciences, and as a means for the further development of that kind of work in fields where such development has either been lacking so far, or is weak. In other words, there are two kinds of task that must be carried out in the spirit of science, but which, in the nature of the case, cannot be performed by any single science taken separately. One of these tasks is "putting together the pieces." Each science deals with its own segment of the universe, of existence; but the universe, the totality of existence, is obviously an interconnected affair, each segment of which has vital relationships to other segments. To understand each part properly, it is therefore necessary to form a general picture—a picture that puts the relationships of the parts into meaningful and confirmable perspective. Only in this way is it possible to discover what is common to all the parts, as well as what is more basic and what is less basic.

The other task is to respond to the need for further sciences. If we reckon physical science in its modern sense as having begun with Copernicus' heliocentric conception of the planetary system, then it is only a few hundred years old, while social and behavioral sciences are still younger. Just as philosophy gave rise to new sciences in the past, so it will have a continuing opportunity to do so in the future. And it will never render itself obsolete, for the more this task of helping to bring into being new and separate sciences is carried out, the greater becomes philosophy's other task of synthesizing and generalizing their results.

6. *Marxist materialism says that it does not wish to deny true existence to ideas and ideals, which are not themselves material; it only maintains that such forms of existence arise out of matter. But how could matter produce something that is not material?*

By functioning; one must remember that matter—all matter, in whatever form—is active, not passive. To exist is to be in process, through the exercise of forces, powers, energies. Seeing a tree is a complex process, which produces an image that is not material in the same sense as the tree is. Memory is a still more complex process; it gives rise to a sort of image of an image, which is even less material than the original visual image. Abstraction is a still more complex process, which gives rise to a sort of image of a part or aspect of an image—a part or aspect that is never found by itself, such as the height of the tree. Height, as an abstract idea, is not material; but there can be no doubt that it is arrived at through the functioning of sense organs, nerve networks and brain cells that are material. Through repeated observation and experiment, we have located and traced many of the processes involved.

The ideals of universal peace and justice, as ideals, are not material. But they have no meaning or existence except in terms of the senses, the brain, and the nervous system going through various processes of functioning, which we call feeling, memory, abstraction, imagination, and the like. We see what war is like; we feel and remember its pain and anguish; we imagine a future without it.

7. *If the creation of ideals is explained in terms of the functioning of physiological organs, nervous systems, and brain structures, which in turn are explained as complex forms of development of primary matter, doesn't this amount to saying that the simpler and the lower are capable of creating the complex and the higher? Isn't this unlikely and unnatural? Must not the same thing be said of the materialist thesis that inorganic matter gives rise to life, and also to consciousness?*

There is a quite fundamental difference between saying, "The lower *creates* the higher" and "The lower *evolves into* the higher." At one time, the latter possibility may have seemed unlikely and unnatural; but, after the large-scale and detailed confirmation of the validity of the evolutionary approach—first in biology, and then in other fields—that time has come to an end. Likewise, if one-celled organisms can evolve into more complex forms of life, which in turn evolve into so complex a form as man, it no longer seems unlikely or unnatural that the most complex forms of inorganic matter should evolve into the simplest forms of the organic, and that the property of consciousness should develop along with the growing development of living forms. Whenever something simple grows into something complex, there is a sense in which one can assert that the complex must have been potential in the simpler. In that sense, it may be said that all the higher and more complex manifestations in the universe are potential in the simpler units and forms out of which they evolved.

2.

The Nature of Thought:
Logic and Dialectics

We began the preceding chapter with a question difficult for man to answer, but impossible for him to avoid:
What sort of totality is he a part of? As we saw, the
reason that question is basic and unavoidable is that
man is a conscious, thinking creature, who cannot help
feeling the need for an overall orientation, just as he
feels the need for light in strange surroundings. In the
same way in which that question forms the starting
point of ontology, another question, equally basic and
unavoidable for man, deriving also from his very nature
and needs as a thinking animal, forms the starting point
of another part of philosophy (methodology). That is
the question: What is the correct method of thinking?
By what method do we arrive at the truth?

Every human being is a thinking creature, in the
sense that he or she is capable of conscious mental activity. Of course, some of this activity—such as daydream-
ing, musing, wondering, and the like—may not involve
the question of correct method in any important way.
But the question must be confronted, with all its ur-
gency, when we come to the kind of conscious mental
activity that we associate principally with the word
"thinking"—namely, reasoning, the particular kind of

thinking through which we try to solve problems, to arrive at conclusions that we can prove.

The materialist takes as his point of departure the proposition that the correct method of thought is determined by the nature of things, by the basic properties of existence. This is one of the senses in which Marxists take the traditional formulation: Being determines consciousness. The very word reflection, as used in connection with the thinking process, suggests this point. Just as a physical reflection of something is a sort of copy of certain visible characteristics, so mental reflection is also a kind of attempt to arrive at a correct report about certain things. In the latter case, the things are not usually such that a literal, mechanical copy, or a single act of vision, would satisfy the need, or supply the correct report that is wanted. If we merely wish to ascertain the size or identity of someone who died of a certain disease, a direct look, or the inspection of a photograph, could suffice. But if we want to find out the cause of the disease, the matter cannot be settled so easily; the question of correct method then becomes central.

Another way of putting the problem is to say that we want to discover the laws of correct thinking, the rules and procedures for reaching correct conclusions. This part of philosophy has been traditionally called logic. The problem might thus be adequately expressed by saying that what we want to find out are the laws and rules of logic. However, a confusion easily arises in connection with this way of expressing it, because the term "logic" has become associated with one particular theory, one particular conception of what the laws of correct thinking are. The word "logic" comes from the Greek *logos*, and one of the earliest (and most influential) theories concerning correct thinking and its laws is that developed by Aristotle. This conception, which we shall examine presently, is called "formal logic." Sometimes it is simply called "Aristotelian logic," which is better, because it helps us to remember that this is one theory about the subject matter, and that there are others.

By subject matter we mean in this case correct thinking itself, which of course arose in man as a fact, and was carried on by him in practice long before anyone propounded any theories to try to explain its nature and state its basic laws. We see the same situation in all fields of study. Nature has been going through what we have come to call astronomical, physical, and chemical processes long before anyone tried to explain them in terms of theories and laws; and man was necessarily going through physiological and other processes (including reasoning) prior to the appearance of any theories about them. One source of confusion is that we often use the same word to designate both the subject matter about which we are trying to gain correct knowledge, and the correct knowledge that we think we have gained. Thus we refer, for example, to the physiology, psychology, or logic of a child when we mean the natural subject matter, the actual processes that take place in the child, all of which constitutes one thing, and also when we mean the knowledge that we think we have gained about these processes—which is quite another thing.

What we are emphasizing is that, if we mean by "logic itself" the same thing as "actually correct thinking," then we must remember that Aristotelian logic, or what is called in philosophy "formal logic," is not to be identified with "logic itself." If it could be so identified, we could conclude that to question the theories, laws, and explanations offered by textbooks on formal logic would be to call into question the very existence or reality of the process of correct thinking itself. This would be akin to imagining that when Copernicus called into question the Ptolemaic conception of a geocentric planetary system and a fixed earth, he was casting doubt on the earth and the other planets themselves, or that Darwin was casting doubt on plant and animal life itself in challenging the Linnean conception of fixed species, or that Einstein was throwing out moving bodies themselves when he departed from Newtonian explanations of motion. When it is said, "After all, there is one biology, one logic," we must be careful about the sense in which this is true. There is, indeed, one set of actual facts, one state of affairs that is objectively the case in either field. But there are certainly different and competing theories, different conceptions and laws offered in the continuing (and let us hope, progressing) effort to explain the facts.

The best way to understand the position of Marxist philosophy on this whole matter is to examine the basic laws of thought as they were conceived by Aristotle, and then to contrast these with the conception presented by Marx and Engels. It will then become clear that on both sides, the judgment as to what are the laws of correct thinking is dependent on what are taken to be the basic characteristics of existence, so that the issue at the methodological level goes back to a difference at the ontological level.

The Aristotelian conception of the laws basic to correct thinking may be stated as follows:

1. *Law of Identity: Each existence is identical with itself. A is A.*

2. *Law of Noncontradiction: Each existence is not different from itself. A is not non-A.*[1]

3. *Law of Excluded Middle: No existence can be both itself and different from itself. Any X is either A or non-A, but not both at once.*

It is evident that these laws represent attempts to state the basic nature of existence, and to use that as the key to the correct method of thinking. This is in no way a strange or unnatural approach, since thinking is always thinking about something that in some way exists, even if only as a fiction in the mind; and correct thinking must be thinking that properly reflects, faithfully follows out, the characteristics and properties of what it is dealing with.

It is also quite evident that what Aristotle sees as the most basic characteristic of existence is static self-identity. His three laws really make the same point from three different angles: positively, by saying that a thing can be only what it is; negatively, by saying that a thing cannot be what it is not; and dichotomously, by saying that there are only two alternatives—to be A or not to be A—and they are mutually exclusive.

All these propositions seem to most of us to be mere truisms, seem to be so plainly self-evident that any possibility of seriously questioning or challenging them is practically precluded. However, the Marxist would hold that we have these views chiefly because we are so conditioned by our type of education, that any other views on the question are seldom if ever brought to anyone's attention. As this kind of situation has arisen a great many times in the history of thought, we should be open-minded. Most Marxists have felt not only that there is a need to challenge this conception of the basic nature of existence and of correct thinking, but also that, when the issue is seriously examined in the light of the evidence, it will be seen that this conception is inadequate because it is oversimplified. In passing, it is interesting and important to note that Marx and Engels were not the first to present such a challenge. They found the essence of it in their immediate predecessor, Hegel, while the seeds of it were clearly discernible in the work of Heraclitus more than 2,000 years earlier.

The essence of the challenge is that this conception of the nature of existence and thought does not sufficiently take into the account the fact of continuous change. If something is in process of continuous change in all its parts all the time, can it be properly spoken of as if it were in fact self-identical? Will the truth about it best be found by accepting a rule of thinking that says it must be so considered? Such a rule, though very useful to a degree, and in relation to certain kinds of problems, places obstacles in the way of understanding and dealing with change, of solving problems connected with pervasive and underlying changes, especially qualitative ones. Hence, Marx and Engels held that these Aristotelian conceptions tell some truth, but that what they tell amounts to a limited and partial story; yet they tell that story as if it were full and complete, as if there were nothing important to add to it.

Let us take the simple instance of a piece of paper. According to Aristotle's laws, the paper is the paper (A is A); it is not different from the paper (A is not non-A); and anything that exists must either be that paper or not

be that paper. However, if we watch the paper closely
enough and long enough, we have to question whether it
is actually following these laws. We know that after
thousands of years, even though no one has so much as
touched the piece of paper, it would be very different
from what it is now. In fact, it would not be paper.

It would have changed chemically and physically to
such an extent that it would be something else. In ordinary speech we would say perhaps that it crumbled into
dust. The point is that everything is all the while busy
becoming something else. For if we raise the question,
"When do the changes take place by which the paper is
becoming dust? by which the seed is becoming a plant?
by which the child is becoming an adult?" the answer is,
of course, that they are taking place all of the time. And
the more we examine the changing object, the more we
are forced to the conclusion that the changes involved
are not only taking place all the time, but in all parts of
the object.

Although to superficial inspection the paper may seem
inert, scientific examination discloses a scene of tremendous activity, of pervasive dynamism and change. The
paper is seen to be mostly "empty space," in which
there are billions of whirling, charged particles, which
form changing series of combinations of various kinds.
The empty space itself must not be thought of as nothingness, but as a field possessed of definite properties. All
these things and events—the billions of highly activized
particles, the field that has certain effects on them, the
positive and negative forces at work, the opposing combinations of units pushing and pulling in different directions—all this is not something that takes place *on* the
paper; it *is* the paper. The seemingly calm surface is

something like a seething cauldron which we are looking at from a distance, and which for that reason appears to be still.

If all this is so, then how can we use the paper as paper? If it is changing in all its parts all the time, how can we recognize it as paper? The answer lies in the *rate* of change. When the total rate, the net effect in relation to the object as a whole, is not too rapid, the paper is usable for a sufficiently long period. But how can we use it at all, if it is mostly empty space, in which shifting combinations of energized particles are whirling at tremendous velocities? How could a pencil make an identifiable mark on it? You cannot write on the surface of a seething cauldron. But you could, if the net effect of the pressures and motions within, no matter how great they were, resulted in a sufficiently slow rate of change *in toto*, or "at the surface." It is then like a tug of war, where tremendous forces are exerted on either side, resulting in a slow, overall progression in one direction. To make another comparison, a volcano might have tremendous activity internally, manifesting itself at a relatively distant surface in a stream of lava moving slowly enough for people to be able to imprint their initials and to read them for weeks or months, as they read them for seconds or minutes after marking them in the moist sand at the seashore.

But still, how is even this possible, if the very object with which one tries to make the mark—a pencil, a stick, or one's finger—is itself mostly empty space, in which there is the same kind of whirling aggregate of infinitesimally tiny particles? Doesn't something have to remain "still," and "solid"? The answer is "no." Again, much depends on the *rate* of motion and change. A swarm of particles, if it moves around rapidly enough *within* the area occupied by the swarm, creates the effect of a solid screen. Something that represents a weaker aggregate of forces, upon coming into contact with such a screen, is repelled. Of course, this something is also a swarm that creates the effect of a solid screen. It is a case of one rapidly whirling group bumping into another rapidly whirling group. Two such groups, upon approaching each other, and accommodating their total or net changes to each other for certain purposes (such as one writing on the other), can form an interrelating system in which one can regard the other as "still," in the same way as two persons who are traveling side by side in different high speed vehicles might shake hands with each other (one of them might even sign an autograph book held "still" by the other).

These are some of the factors that enter into the paradoxical but pervasive dynamics whereby each thing is busy changing itself, is in process of becoming something else twenty-four hours a day. The dialectical materialist holds that, in a universe in which everything is formed of units of this kind, the basic rules of correct thinking should reflect the basic situation, which is not one wherein the static, the changeless, is at the core and essence of things, while change plays only a secondary or superficial role, but rather one in which change is of the essence and at the core, while it is the "stabilities" that are passing and temporary. The process whereby each thing is changing its identity is primary, continuous, and absolute; it is the identities reached that are secondary, temporary, and relative.

What are the laws of correct thinking, according to the dialectical materialist? What would be put in place of the Aristotelian principles? As in the case of Aristotle, the laws that he arrives at are as much ontological as methodological. That is, they are statements of what he considers to be the most general and basic characteristics of existence, and for that very reason statements also of the most basic and determining factors in correct thinking. Like Aristotle's, they are three in number.

The first is usually called the Law of Strife, Interpenetration, and Unity of Opposites. It may be expressed in the formula, A is A and also non-A. This law represents a summation of much of our previous discussion: first, in respect to the ontological problem of what is common and basic to all existence; second, in respect to the methodological problem of how to think correctly, so as to solve problems that of necessity deal with existence. Let us consider these two aspects in turn.

Ontologically, the general point may be put as follows: The reason each thing is actually in process of change in all its parts all the time is that each "thing" is made up of opposing forces and differently acting elements. These are called "opposites," in the same sense as that in which any forces or elements that are different from each other, exerting themselves in different directions or toward different ends in the same field, may be designated as opposites. The differing forces, or the differing elements, do not exist simply side by side, like neighbors each of whom goes his own way without having any vital relationships to the other. If that were the case, no complex "thing" would be formed that we would be likely to identify with a name, no "unity" of elements would emerge. The opposing forces and the different elements interpenetrate to form a closely knit pattern that hangs together, that maintains itself as a pattern for a sufficient period of time to be distinguishable, recognizable, usable in some way as a thing or unity —an object, a property, a concept.

This is what accounts for the fact that everything has a history. Everything changes, grows, develops into something else, not only because it is affected in some way by some other thing from the outside, but also because the very components out of which each thing is made—and their interrelationships within the thing— are such as to force changes. Change is thus a built-in condition, not only of physical and chemical "things," but of existences at every level—including the human, the social, the moral, esthetic, and logical levels.

It is perhaps not necessary to dwell on the point that man is a creature made up of tendencies, impulses, desires, instincts, and the like, which pull him in different directions, which represent processes and changes within him, which keep him "on the go." Even when he is "resting," the changes, of course, go on. Not only does individual man undergo the processes of constant movement and change; the species man, as a species, is also in motion—as a product of, and in process of, evolution.

It is probably also unnecessary to emphasize the fact that a society, as a society, is in continuous process of change because it is made up of diverse and conflicting elements, is possessed of forces that pull it and push it in different directions. There are groups whose interests are bound up with maintaining certain existing institutions; at the same time there are groups whose interests are bound up with eliminating those institutions. New ideas are constantly appearing, and are constantly being resisted. Pressures are exerted on the society from both outside and inside. New needs are created, which result in new demands and new patterns of behavior. New opportunities are discovered, thus stimulating new types of activity. Any society must, of course, be enough of a unity to remain together, with sufficient consensus and cooperation to function as a society. It must attain a certain equilibrium; but this is plainly a dynamic equilibrium, in which every successive unity, every status quo, is temporary, while the struggle of opposing forces is continuous.

However, even if all this be admitted, the question still arises: Is this really intended to apply also to ideas, to concepts, to moral and esthetic values? What sort of evidence can the dialectical materialist adduce in support of the thesis that such forms of existence as these are also scenes of the strife of interpenetrating opposites, which form unities that are not permanent, but temporary? As an example, let us take an idea, the abstract idea of constitutionality.

We may ordinarily think of this, or of any other idea, as a unit; but we realize upon reflection that this unit is made up of different elements, interrelated in a certain way. In fact, the very definition of an idea is a statement of some of the chief elements and types of relationship present. Let us take the following definition of constitutionality: the logical compatibility of a law or an action with the provisions of a constitution. We see at once that this idea would not—could not—exist except as a combination of elements, which are themselves other ideas, or aspects of other ideas. This is, of course, very similar to the way in which material things are made up of different combinations of material units.

In other words, if we did not understand the idea of logical compatibility, that of law, and that of constitution itself, we would not be able to understand the idea of constitutionality, just as, if we could not physically identify hydrogen and oxygen, we would not be able to put them together in a certain proportion in order to produce water. Every idea has specific *content* as an idea, quite apart from the fact that it also represents an abstraction from material things. We are speaking here, not of the relation of ideas to material things, but of the relation of idea parts to idea wholes. That ideas arise out of matter and the functioning of matter is the *materialism* side of the story. The content and internal dynamics of ideas as ideas is the *dialectical* side of the story. In strict terminology, dialectical materialism is the ontology, materialist dialectics the methodology.

It is clear, then, that a particular idea is composed of idea elements that are joined in a certain definite relationship. It is also clear that this relationship does not represent a mere juxtaposition, without vital jointure, but is an interpenetration. These idea elements must in various ways and degrees overlap, coalesce, coincide; they must be identical, yet different. "Logical compatibility" must be present in constitutionality, but is not restricted to it, and therefore includes much more than constitutionality; the latter is thus a part of the former. What distinguishes this part from the other parts is that it is concerned only with government-related actions and laws. Aristotle long ago emphasized that definition consists in relating the idea to be defined (termed the "species") to a "genus" (the next more inclusive idea of which the species is a part), and to what he called the "specific difference," the characteristics that set the particular species off from the rest of the genus.

But Aristotle conceived of these relationships in a

static sense. He held that ideas, as ideas, could not move or change, and if they did, we would not then be able to think correctly about them. The dialectician holds that this position is far too sweeping, that it would really mean that ideas, as ideas, do not have a history. But the fact is that they do. The most he can therefore agree to, along these lines, is that there are some problems that can be correctly solved while one disregards the changes that are taking place. Nevertheless, they do take place, and in other problems they become crucial.

Aristotle appears to have thought that, while we may move from one idea to another, the ideas themselves are static, like the primary aspects of reality, in his conception of reality. This is essentially the same view as that taken of biological species prior to Darwin's work: the species exist side by side, but all are fixed; none grew out of others. The dialectician holds that there is no more reason for taking this view in the case of ideas than there is in the case of animals, although he notes that, when a view of this kind is taken in one field, it influences and encourages the taking of it in another. In any case, he points to the fact that such ideas as "logical agreement," "constitution," "law," and the like, undergo radical changes during the course of time; and he maintains that it is better, in a scientific sense, to explain a process of this kind as a growth or evolution than to deal with it as an unexplained transition between unaltered entities.

The way in which ideas grow is evident; the elements that compose them cannot help but be affected by new discoveries of fact, new approaches, new insights, responses to new situations, and thus they undergo change. Such changes in one element or another of those that make up an idea represent a logical pressure, which modifies the idea as a whole, and moves the total complex in a certain direction—a process that calls for adjustment by the other elements. We associate all this with progress; but progress, which gives change a central role, was not a leading concept in the systems of classical thinkers, like Aristotle or Plato.

We see basically the same situation at the level of esthetic conceptions, and in relation to the content of works of art. Standards of what is beautiful or not beautiful evidently undergo historical changes, a fact now so taken for granted that it may be regarded as a truism. There would no longer seem to be any serious dispute as to whether it is proper to say that esthetic concepts have a history. The only important issue is how to explain this history, what to trace it to, what its primary causes are. It is also a truism that works of art have their own internal dynamics, that they represent essentially tensions of some kind that have been brought to a resolution, conflicting elements and forces reaching some kind of unity. "Strife, interpenetration, and unity of opposites" is indeed a description that might literally fit almost any work of art.

In short, the first law of thought, as seen by materialist dialectics, represents (like the others) a generalization, the aim of which is to sum up what is found to be common to every level of existence. The essence of the generalization is that, in order to think correctly, we must bear in mind that any existence we are dealing with is a changing unity, the result of the fact that it is made up of opposing dynamic constituents in dynamic interrelationships. The fact that some problems can be adequately handled without reference to the changes that are taking place must not mislead us into thinking that we are dealing with unchanging unities.

If the first law thus expresses the fact that everything has a history, the second expresses the fact that this history is not only quantitative, but qualitative. We may formulate it as the Law of Transition from Quantity to Quality (that is from Quantitative Changes of Old Qualities to New Qualities). To understand this law, we must bear in mind that any change that takes place in anything is first of all a change in degree, a quantitative change in those qualities that at present enter into the make-up of the thing. (The term "qualities," of course, denotes the basic characteristics and properties of things.)

When we increase the temperature of water, within certain limits, we witness a quantitative change. The water remains water: it retains its basic character of a liquid; but it becomes a hotter liquid. However, if the quantitative change continues—that is, if the temperature of the water continues to be raised—a transition to a gaseous state, a new qualitative condition, takes place. Steam is not simply hotter water with an increased degree of the properties of water; it has new properties that are not possessed by water. So, too, when the temperature of the liquid, water, is decreased, the result—within a certain range—is a colder liquid; if the temperature is lowered beyond a certain point, however, a qualitative change takes place, this time to a solid—ice. Again, the properties of ice are not merely increased or decreased degrees of the properties of water. As a solid, ice possesses properties that water does not.

In other words, what this law is saying is that every accumulation of quantitative changes leads, from time to time in its ongoing course, to new qualities; old qualities are transformed into new ones. It is also saying that this is the only way in which new qualities come into being—as the result of quantitative changes in the old ones. Thus the history that everything undergoes is not a simple, one-dimensional progression, in which later developments can be mechanistically "reduced" to earlier ones, and new qualities can be seen simply as increased or decreased amounts of the qualities earlier present. That is the mechanical "reductive fallacy," which the dialectician urges us to avoid.

If we do not avoid it, then we are led along deceptive paths, like that of treating the child as if he were simply a small adult, or the adult as if he were simply a larger child. Or, in the same vein, we may imagine that, if we admit that the species man developed out of lower animal species, we are then asserting that man possesses nothing but greater or lesser amounts of the characteristics of lower animals. In other words, we may think we see things that are not really there (as when it was seriously taught that microscopic examination revealed the human germ cell to be a tiny model of a person, with limbs and other parts of the body simply reduced in size), or we may think that what we see cannot possibly be there (as when the evidence for biological evolution was denied).

When we put together what is asserted in the first and second laws, we confront the most basic and controversial aspect of the materialist dialectical position— that is, its conclusion that what formal logic has called "contradictory" (and therefore impossible) exists objectively in nature (and must therefore be reflected in logical patterns that in some way go beyond those of formal logic). What must be taken into account is the fact that, when an existence is in process of changing, it is not in process of becoming more of the same thing; it is in process of becoming something else—something not that thing. A piece of paper, a mountain, a child, a social order like feudalism—these are not things changing into more paper, more mountain, more child, more feudalism. What, then, does it actually mean for paper to be paper, for mountain to be mountain, for child to be child, for feudalism to be feudalism? It means to keep on changing into something else.

If everything is like that, if every A is an entity that is continuously changing into non-A, then A is non-A as much as it is A. Surely a thing *is* what it is constantly changing *into*, as much as what it is constantly changing *from*. If this seems to formal logic to be so paradoxical as to be utterly impossible, that is because formal logic was based on an oversimplified view of what is happening in the natural order of things, because it mistook one part of the story for the whole story. It thought the story had an ending.

The reply of the formal logician has always been that the laws of Identity and of Noncontradiction (A is A, and cannot be non-A) apply to a given instant of time, that he (the formal logician) realizes that things do eventually change, but is pointing to the fact that *at a given instant* the given A is and can be only A, is static at that instant, and must be thought of as such. The dialectical logician, in turn, replies to this argument by pointing out that it would be a good one—if we could find such instants of time. But the fact is that we cannot. The instants of time we actually do find are not instants *at* which the existence in question ceases to change, is held in static suspension, but are instants *during* which changes go on in all parts of the thing. In other words, the tiniest instant of time is still an interval during which something is happening; and what is happening is that the given A is in process of becoming non-A, though for the time it may be said to be more A than non-A. What we have in the smallest instant is an A that is also non-A just because it is A, because there is no other way to be A. This means the true A contains contradiction in its very essence.

It is important to notice that this position does not represent a denial of the truth of the proposition that A is A. It is not that formal logic was wrong in every sense. It went wrong in asserting that, because A was A, there was no sense in which it could justifiably be said that A was also simultaneously non-A. The formal conception of identity is that the A that is A is an A from which contradiction is excluded. The dialectical conception of identity is that the A which is A includes contradiction.

It is around this point that some of the most interesting controversies of contemporary Marxists have centered. Broadly speaking, three approaches can be distinguished:

1. The conceptions of formal logic can be accepted as applying only to relations of thought, to ideas, not things. Dialectical principles apply to things; but formal logic must be left standing as the only valid logic, the only valid way of correct thinking. There is no need for the concept of a dialectical *logic*.

2. The basic statements of formal logic, such as the laws of Identity and Noncontradiction, can be accepted provided they are interpreted in a dialectical sense. That is, the principle of Identity is met in such a formulation

as: "An A that is in process of changing into non-A is an A that is in process of changing into non-A"; and the principle of Noncontradiction is met by acknowledging, indeed insisting, that it cannot be denied that an A changing in that way *is* changing in that way. Thus logic becomes dialectical if we interpret formal logic in a certain way, but there is no need to speak of formal logic and dialectical logic.

3. The "classical" approach, taken by Engels, asserts that both formal and dialectical logic must be recognized; that the former possesses limited and relative validity, the latter a deeper and more inclusive validity; that the latter therefore asserts principles which go beyond, and contradict principles asserted by the former.

The chief points of difference may be seen in relation to what Engels said about motion. He wrote:

> So long as we consider things as static and lifeless, each one by itself, along side of and after each other, it is true that we do not run up against any contradictions in them. . . . But the position is quite different as soon as we consider things in their motion, their change, their life, their reciprocal influence on one another. Then we immediately become involved in contradictions. Motion itself is a contradiction; even simple mechanical change of place can only come about through a body at one and the same moment of time being both in one place and in another place, being in one and the same place and also not in it. And the continuous assertion and simultaneous solution of this contradiction is precisely what motion is.[2]

According to the first variant that is found among contemporary Marxists, Engels was simply mistaken about the nature of motion, having been unduly influenced by Hegel, among others. He should not have gone so far as to say that a body in motion is "in one and the same place and also not in it." He should have contented himself with saying that a moving body is "both in one place and in another place." Had he stopped there, he would have stopped short of insisting upon the existence of what is logically contradictory. Being in one place *and in another place* at the same time is not logically contradictory, since body possesses extension, among other properties. But to be in *one* place and yet *not* in that place is contradiction, and as such, inadmissible.

This approach maintains that there is only one logic, formal logic; and that all the changes, motions, and evolutionary developments that are found in nature can be adequately expressed in terms of the categories and rules of formal logic. This by no means represents either a rejection of dialectical principles, or a denial of the pervasive existence of quantitative and qualitative changes, or of the need to seek further for such changes in every field, including that of the history of logic itself. But the contention is that the history and content of logic can be adequately expressed without making the categories of logic dialectical. Thus this approach represents a direct denial of the validity of a number of positions taken by Marx and Engels. It is found in all Communist countries today, openly maintained in writing, and by influential philosophers of high academic rank, although the degree of influence that this approach has, relative to the others, varies greatly. In Poland, for example, it represents the predominant tendency; in the Soviet Union, it is a minority position.

The second and third variants, although they differ

on how existing contradictions should be assimilated by logical theory, agree that Engels was right in insisting that contradiction exists as an objective fact in nature, and that motion is an instance of this. Here, it is very important to note precisely what is asserted by Engels (and those who here agree) and what is not asserted. There is no intention to state that, in respect to every proposition that is found to be true, its contradictory will also be found to be true. This would mean that whenever we can truly say, "There is a chair in this room" or, "The author of this book was born in New York City," or, "Two and two make four," we must also say, at the same time, "There is no chair in this room," "The author of this book was not born in New York City," "Two and two do not make four."

To imagine that materialist dialectical logic makes claims of this kind would be the same as to imagine that Engels' analysis of motion maintained that it must be said, at one and the same time, that "The body is moving," and "The body is not moving." As we have seen, Engels did not maintain that. What he did say was, first, that it is true, not false, that a certain body is moving; second, that in this fact, this truth, contradictory elements and relationships—that is, relationships which formal logic defines as contradictory—can be found and therefore must be recognized. That is, the body could not move unless it could be both at a point and not at it during the same instant. Thus, if we are dealing with the problem of the nature of motion, it is necessary to say something contradictory about every moving body. But this does not mean that whenever we say a body is moving, we must also say that it is not moving, irrespective of the kind of problem raised.

Relative to certain problems, such as an explanation of the starting and stopping moments, it might well be necessary to say that there is an instant during which the body is moving and also not moving. But relative to other problems—such as whether the earth is a fixed body, around which all the other astronomical bodies move, or a moving body in the same sense as the others are—the answer is not that it is both a moving body and not a moving body, but simply that it is a moving body. Whether a statement is true naturally depends on its meaning, and its meaning is always relative to a given context of discourse. The dialectical position is not that every true statement *as meant* is a statement whose contradictory must be equally true, but that there are certain statements that, as meant, are statements whose contradictories turn out to be equally true upon careful examination. In short, the position is not that all contradictions that can be stated must exist, but rather that all that exists contains certain contradictions, which must be recognized if certain important problems are to be solved.

That there is a chair in this room the dialectical logician will say is true, not false; and he will not say that the proposition, "There is no chair in this room," is at the same time also true, unless, indeed, he happens to be speaking about that very instant during which the chair is being taken into, or out of, the room. In other words, it is safe to say that there eventually will be (and that there has already been) such an instant, since the evidence is very strong that there never has been or will be a chair and a room that have existed together, and will exist together, from all eternity to all eternity. But this does not mean that for every situation in which it is true to say, "There is a chair in this room" it is also true to say, "There is no chair in this room." As we have seen, the dialectical logician does say, when the nature of the chair is under discussion, "The chair that is in this room is both chair and non-chair," but that is far from being equivalent to "There is a chair in this room, and at the same time there is no chair in this room."

It is told of Thoreau that when any of his neighbors asked him how he was, or how things were, he was given to launching into such an exhaustive account of how he conceived of his own existence, his assessment of the problems of the state, the nation, and modern man generally, that they left off asking him. The truth about all that is very complex, and needs a long answer; but they were not really asking about all that. So also, while the form that is used to register a copyright has a place to indicate where the author was born, even the most scrupulous honesty does not require that he try to tell the whole dialectical story in his answer to that question. The part of the truth thus asked for can be adequately stated by means of a noncontradictory proposition.

Mathematical propositions are no exception to these dialectical rules. If we are teaching a child simple arithmetic, or making change, the problem as posed is such that its solution is fully expressible in the noncontradictory proposition, "Two and two make four." However, if we were dealing, not with children in the elementary grades, but with philosophers of mathematics, and the problem was whether mathematical entities and mathematical truths do or do not change, grow, evolve, whether they do or do not contain contradictory elements or contradictory relations of any kind, the question would be a different one, and would necessitate a different kind of answer, in order to express the part or aspect of the truth that was then being sought.

One then would have to point out that what is now meant by two and two making four, what is now taught as the meaning of this statement, is quite different from what it was taken to mean when George Washington and Thomas Jefferson went to school. To put the point in a fashion that is perhaps too blunt, yet that suggests the nature of the situation, "Two and two make four" was then taken to be true on the ground that it correctly reported how tangible, observable things related to one another. Mathematical truth had at that time that kind of empirical meaning. Another way of stating the situation would be to point out that everyone at that time was brought up on Bacon and Newton, and had not yet heard of Hume and Russell. Since the work of Hume and Russell, "Two and two make four" has taken on (for many) a nonempirical meaning, one whose truth is considered to be independent of how things behave.

The materialist dialectician holds that this represents a qualitative change, a change from A to non-A (from "Mathematical truth is empirically grounded" to "Mathematical truth is not empirically grounded"). This is the process of the growth and evolution of ideas as ideas—a process which, he maintains, can be understood and explained only by recognizing the presence of opposing, contradictory elements in the ideas, and the fact that changes of degree in these elements can lead to qualitative changes. After all, if the process of quantitative accumulations giving rise to new qualities did not take place also within mathematical ideas as ideas, then the sum of two odd numbers, one and one, would not produce an even number, but simply a number twice as odd as one.

We must not be deceived by the fact that we use the same words, into thinking that we are still saying the same thing, if the meaning of the words is meanwhile undergoing change. In short, in terms of what is meant by "Two and two make four," there are moments and problems in the history of mathematics in relation to which one may well have to say, "While it is true that two and two make four, it is at the same time not true that two and two make four." However, dialectical logic does not make the mistake of saying that all contradictory propositions must be true; but formal logic makes the mistake of saying that no contradictory proposition can be true.

The third dialectical law is called "Negation of the Negation." The terminology in which all these laws are traditionally expressed is that of nineteenth-century German philosophy, but their meaning can be put into more familiar language without great difficulty. The term "negation" was used to designate the new state or condition into which something grows. Since this growth represents a passage from the old state or condition, the new state is considered a negation of the old. Thus the emergence of every new quality constitutes a "negation" of something that was previously present. The point of this law is that the story does not end there; quantitative changes continue with respect to the new quality as well. In time, the accumulation of these changes results in the breakup of that quality, and the emergence of a further one. Thus the previous negation is in turn negated, and there is no evidence of the possibility of a terminal point in this process of new qualities arising out of old.

In brief, the first law says that everything has a history; the second, that the history is qualitative as well as quantitative; the third, that this kind of history does not stop. It is very important to bear in mind that all these laws are presented as conclusions that are arrived at on the basis of the factual evidence found at all levels of existence. They are not presented as a priori principles, whose truth or validity is independent of experience.

Since these patterns of change are found in everything, and there is no evidence that anything remains immune to change, it is felt that they must be accepted as universal principles, valid at this stage of universal history, until different evidence is forthcoming. The position taken is one of willingness to modify any one of them in the light of objective evidence—*if* there is such evidence. Furthermore, it must be emphasized that, even though these principles are regarded as empirical generalizations, it is not claimed that the specific laws of change at each level of existence can be predicted or deduced from them. All that is deducible or predictable is that quantitative and qualitative patterns of change will be found, that contradictions are present at each level. But what the specific laws are—the laws peculiar to the content of that level—what is the specific content of the contradictions, cannot be stated in advance. Such matters can be determined only by specific factual investigations.

However, investigations never take place in a methodological vacuum. They must have a basic guide and perspective; and this must come from a summation of what has been found so far in the picture as a whole. That

summation must represent what might be termed the
most scientific account that can be given of what is basic
to the methods of science. The Marxist philosopher does
not seek to *add* something to scientific method; he seeks
to base himself on what is contained in it.

What, then, is his view of the nature of truth? For
him, the most important characteristic of truth is that it
is objective. The Marxist materialist wishes to distinguish his position from voluntarism, the tendency to
make truth dependent on the will of man; from any
form of subjectivism, which would make truth dependent on how we think, rather than the other way around;
and from pragmatism, which, in basing truth on utility,
sets up too relativistic a concept of truth. The dialectical
materialist recognizes that there is indeed a relativistic
element in truth, especially as it enters into knowledge,
and he stresses the relationship between truth and practical utility, practice. But his conception is that, while
human knowledge at any given stage must always be
relative, in the sense that it cannot be complete, there
does exist an objective (dynamic) state of affairs, which
is whatever it is, in an absolute sense. It is this that
determines the content of true knowledge and the utility that true knowledge possesses for man. Practice is the
criterion by which man comes to know that the truth *is*
the truth, but it is not what *makes* the truth the truth.

It is important also to emphasize that when Marxism
refers to a "class approach" to the search for truth, the
"class significance" of doctrines, or the "party spirit"
that enters into philosophy, it is not thereby casting any
doubt on the objectivity of truth. It is expressing the
fact that historical developments can reach a point at
which the material interests of certain classes would be

furthered, and their power retained or enhanced, by clinging to outmoded conceptions, while the interests and power of other classes would be furthered by recognizing and accepting newly discovered truth, by vigorously searching for new truth. This does not mean that whatever. would be in the interests of certain classes must be true, or that people who belong to the right party must always be right.

"Party spirit" enters philosophy and the search for truth, not only consciously, but unconsciously as well. This spirit is not necessarily manifested in deliberate distortions, or attempts to deceive, but in matters of emphasis, in the selection of problems to be worked upon, in the general tone adopted, and in like ways. The "party" significance is seen not only in the form of a motive or intent, but in the actual consequences, relative to the given situation, of the operation of such factors as selection, omission, emphasis, silence, who or what is or is not given "the benefit of the doubt," and so on.

Some of the rules or directives that the dialectical approach to logic would offer in order to guide thinking and to increase the degree of its correctness might be formulated along the following lines:

1. It is not fruitful to assume that the subject matter of any problem can be handled as if it were static, until concrete examination has established that the rate and volume of changes involved are insignificant in relation to the specific nature of the given problem. Only if they are insignificant in that sense will an approach within the confines of the principles of formal logic, as traditionally interpreted, be adequate. Where dialectical principles enter, one should be careful to avoid the fallacy of thinking that all violations of such formal princi-

ples as the Law of Noncontradiction constitute good dialectical reasoning.

2. In dealing with change, one should raise such concrete questions as: Where has this subject matter come from, and where is it going? What were the circumstances of the origin of its present form? What are the main lines along which it is now changing, in regard to concrete content and rate? In other words, one should consider the subject matter in terms of its evolutionary path of development; one should try to see it in relation to what it was and what it is likely to become. This will promote understanding, facilitate prediction, and forestall surprises.

3. In order to understand the evolutionary path of development of any subject matter, one should try to locate within it interpenetrating, contending, opposing elements and forces. Investigate as closely and concretely as possible the nature of the conflict of forces involved; gauge the direction in which the several basic elements tend to move; determine which are stronger and which are weaker. In that way, one will understand better why their conflict is resolved in the way in which it is at present resolved, and how it is likely to be resolved in the future.

4. Be prepared not only for quantitative changes, but also for qualitative ones, in the subject matter. Experience shows that an accumulation of quantitative changes normally results in the emergence of new qualities. This fact should not be resisted as if it were unthinkable, suspect, or mysterious.

5. To the extent that change and development are important in the given problem, the interconnections and interrelationships that necessarily accompany and

underlie development become important. Look for such factors, even when the subject matter seems to be independent or monolithic, and follow them out.

6. When dealing with doctrines, schools of philosophy, social concepts, and the like, bear in mind that their meaning and significance can be gauged only in relation to concrete conditions of time, place, and circumstance. Meaning is conditioned by context; context is dynamic.

QUESTIONS and REPLIES

1. *What is the difference, if any, between the expressions "dialectical materialsm" and "materialist dialectics"?*

The first expression is used to indicate the basic *ontological* theory. Materialism is an ontological doctrine; the adjective "dialectical" distinguishes one form of materialist ontology from others that are not dialectical (e.g., mechanistic materialism, as in Holbach, Diderot, Hobbes, and others). The second expression indicates the basic *methodological* theory. Dialectics is a methodological doctrine; the adjective "materialist" distinguishes one form of dialectical methodology from others which are not materialist (idealist dialectics, as in Hegel).

2. *Is not the whole approach of materialist dialectics an instance of the fallacy of circularity in reasoning? That is, dialectical materialism maintains that the principles of correct thinking can be determined only in the light*

of the basic characteristics of existence, as found by in-
vestigations confirmed in practice. Yet in order to find
and to confirm such generalizations about existence in
its different forms, we must already be in possession of
correct methods of thinking. Is not this, therefore, a
case of assuming all along what we are supposed to be
proving on the basis of evidence?

This criticism fails to take into account the distinction between possessing something, and being able to
explain the thing or function possessed. Man thinks correctly about manifold aspects of his world, and his
thinking is confirmed, by his practice, long before he
raises and tries to solve the problem of how he does this
—that is, of what principles are basic to the process of
thinking correctly. He does not first need to formulate
the laws of correct thinking in order to think correctly,
any more than he first needs to formulate the laws of
vision in order to see correctly, or the laws of digestion
in order to digest well. Man thinks, sees, and digests; in
each case, through actual practice, he necessarily distinguishes, on the basis of results, between what is successful and unsuccessful, correct and incorrect.

What obviously happens is that some attempts to see,
think, and digest come to grief, while others do not.
That makes the difference felt as a fact, and it gives rise
to the question of theory: What is present in those cases
that do not come to grief, that are successful in practice,
as distinguished from those that come to grief, that are
not successful in practice? When the theoretical question is properly answered—that is, when an explanation,
confirmed in practice, is found—the answer will have a
helpful relation to further seeing, thinking, and digest-

ing. Once in possession of basic explanations, we can better deal with cases of faulty practice by preventive or curative measures, as well as strengthen present successful practice, because we now know more than we knew before about what causes failure and success. Just as there is no paradox in the fact that man uses vision in order to discover the laws of vision, knowledge of which in turn is used to improve vision, so also there is no paradox in the fact that man uses reason to discover the laws of reason, knowledge of which in turn is used to improve reasoning.

3. *Since we have scientific method, what need is there for dialectics? What does this add to scientific method?*

Nothing—except an explanation. The problem of explaining scientific method is the problem of trying to discover the basic characteristics that are common to the methods of all the sciences. No one science, and no specialized scientist as such, tries to do this. It requires a synthetic, overall approach and viewpoint. Such philosophers as Aristotle, Bacon, Comte, and John Stuart Mill have dealt with this problem, and have offered such explanations of scientific method. Marxist philosophers maintain that dialectical concepts afford the most satisfactory explanation.

4. *If we lay down principles as broad as those of dialectics—to the effect, for example, that all things without exception change quantitatively and qualitatively in endless sequences—are we not actually settling things by fiat, or by definition? That is, even if future findings appear to be in violation of such principles, we shall say: If*

we continue to look long enough and hard enough, we
shall find these patterns of change. In other words, we
shall never be prepared to say of anything that it violates
these principles. Is it not true, therefore, that we shall be
operating not on the basis of proof, but of assumptions?

In a sense, but not an unwarranted or illegitimate
sense, the process described does take place. That is,
whenever principles are confirmed by a vast mass of past
experience (as in the case also of the principle of casual-
ity—that there can be no effect without a cause), they
are taken as operative hypotheses in dealing with future
experience. But what is of decisive importance to methodology is not the psychological fact that a certain hypothesis is the one chosen to work upon in order to solve
the given problem, but the fact that this hypothesis
shows itself to be *provable* time after time, in different
concrete contexts. If neither proof nor disproof were
forthcoming in the concrete contexts, the situation
would be different, and the hypothesis vulnerable. In
other words, when certain principles (laws of change or
of causation) have been proved by many past cases, we
have more logical warrant to use them as hypotheses for
future cases than to use their contraries. Of course, this
does not obviate the necessity of finding, in each new
case, the *specific* cause, the *concrete* pattern of change.
Until this is done, the new problem is not specifically
solved.

5. *If we say that principles of correct thinking should*
recognize or incorporate contradiction, isn't this some-
thing like saying that a good writer, in describing a con-
fused situation, should write in a confused way? Or, to

put the same question differently: Even though you are observing moving objects, do you not need fixed points of observation in order to tell the truth about the motions?

The answer of Marxist philosophy to the first way of putting the question is that the writer should not write in a confused way. He must describe the confusion clearly, but he must not oversimplify it into something from which confusion is absent. He might, through oversimplification, obtain a result that was very clear; but such clarity would have been purchased at the price of truth.

The answer to the second way of putting the question is that the point of observation one needs in order to tell the truth about motions does not have to be fixed; it is never in fact really fixed. All motions are relative, in that all things are moving. What we need to know (and it is all that we have in fact found out) about the rate of motion of any moving body is the rate observed when calculations are made in relation to something that is regarded as fixed, but which we know is in fact itself in motion. In other words, the truth about rates of motion is always an accurate report relative to a common standard, such as a line drawn on the ground, or a tree standing upright. It is not required that the line or the tree be actually motionless, but only that the same line or the same tree be used under the same conditions. (We know in fact that both the line and the tree, as things fixed to the earth, have an extremely high rate of speed through space.)

This does not mean that all motion is relative, in the sense that there is nothing absolute about it. What is absolute is that motions are taking place, and that bodies are being separated in time and place. The absolute that is here recognized is dynamic, not static.

6. If formal logic remains adequate to certain problems, does this then mean that there are two kinds of truth—one formal and one dialectical?

It would be better to say that there are two aspects of truth here involved, one of which includes the other. Dialectical logic makes room for formal logic within it, much as chemistry makes room for physics and builds on it, or higher mathematics makes room for lower mathematics and builds on it. In other words, dialectical logic recognizes that formal logic is telling part of the truth, in the same way in which we might say that motion pictures can acknowledge that "still" pictures tell part of the truth. In this connection, it is also important to note that a motion picture utilizes and builds upon still pictures in order to do more justice to the actual facts—the facts of motion—than still pictures can.

7. To distinguish between statements that have rational meaning and those that do not, some philosophers (positivists and others) have suggested the following rule: If any statement purporting to be factually true is such that there is by definition—that is, by the very content of the statement—no conceivable set of facts that could ever refute it, then it is without meaning or sense. An example would be: "Everything happens according to the will of God, a will that man cannot claim to understand." Since this statement is compatible with anything that happens, so that no future happening, irrespective of its character, could disprove it, neither could any happening, now or in the future, irrespective of its character, ever prove it. Thus it is classed as a statement that has no rational, cognitive meaning or sense, even though at first glance it seems to have. In the light of these considerations, the question arises: Are not the three laws offered by the materialist dialectician of this same character, since no matter what happens in the future, he will always search within it for the dynamic patterns expressed by these laws?

As was pointed out in the answer to Question 4, the difference is that in separate, concrete cases (such as whether species change, or whether chemical elements are immutable, or whether the earth is fixed), it is possible by objective evidence to *disprove* the old, static view, and to *prove* the dynamic view. (The logical validity of the proof as such has nothing to do with the psychological willingness or unwillingness of the investigator to consider that his hypothesis might have been mistaken.) But, by definition, there is no possibility of proof or disproof about the will of God. The *meaning* in the general principles of dialectics derives from all the separate instances in which the patterns of change have been proved, and from the probability thus created for the continuance of such patterns. New concrete problems are not settled merely by deduction from the general principles, but by testing concrete hypotheses whose meaning is grounded in the possibility of concrete proof or disproof.

PART TWO

Principles
of Social Philosophy

3.

The Nature of Society:
Historical Materialism

The Marxist uses the term "historical materialism" to designate the specifically social part of his philosophy, the part that deals with human society as a whole. The two words composing the term stress the two factors we have found central in his approach from the start: the naturalistic basis (materialism) and the dialectical method (historical). In this case, as we shall see, the word "historical" is doubly appropriate. Not only is the dialectical method in general essentially historical; what is here implied also is that the science of society must be based on a new approach to the discipline traditionally called history.

Let us begin by asking: To what basic problem is the general theory of historical materialism supposed to be the solution? To what questions is it intended to provide the answer? The problem, stated in the overall sense, is to find the basic causal factors that will explain why human history has gone through the particular stages it has gone through up to the present (and, on that basis, to judge its future). In other words, what are the laws of development specific to human history—laws that will account for the path history has actually taken?

The central problem is thus seen in relation to the

general stages through which the history of man has passed. We are of course speaking here not of how man developed out of a species which was not man (that is biological history), but of how the social life of the species man develops, once there is such a species. The earliest stage of social life respecting which we have any considerable evidence is what has sometimes been called the "primitive communal" stage. This precedes the rise of slavery and of any significant development of trade, barter, division of labor, tools of production, or sense of private ownership of the basic sources of production, such as the land. The North American Indians were still predominantly in this stage of development at the time of the first European explorations.

The transition from that type of society to what is sometimes called "slave society" was of very great importance, although it did not take place simultaneously among all peoples who had been living in the primitive communal stage, as may be inferred also from the case of the North American Indians. The rise of slavery is connected with the growth of tools and instruments of production, and with division of labor. Along with these factors goes a deepening, widening, and hardening of the whole idea of private ownership of means of production. Institutions such as written criminal codes, and a permanently organized apparatus of physical enforcement of these codes, also make their appearance.

This general type of slave society flourished in what we call "the world of ancient civilizations"—such as those of Egypt, Greece, Rome, and many others. In the course of time, it gives way to what is termed "feudal society," with which we are most familiar in the medieval development of Western Europe. Slaves are replaced by serfs, slaveowners by hereditary lords. However, the transition that had more significance in terms of our cultural dynamics was from feudalism to what we call "modern capitalism." Gradually, and as a result of tremendous struggles, the hereditary lords, whose power came from their possession of inherited estates and serfs, were displaced as the dominant ruling group by capitalists, whose power was based on industry, trade, and banking. Serfs, as the chief laboring class, were displaced by, or transformed into, free, mobile wageworkers. Today we must add that this system has, at least in part, given way; and that a transition has taken place, in a significant portion of the world, from capitalism to socialism.

It is evident that to study human society is not to study something that exists in a set pattern, and changes only in some superficial or quantitative sense. Society is something going through a process of development that includes qualitative transitions. The institutions which constitute slave society are not simply larger versions of the institutions of primitive communal society, nor is the capitalist society of today a larger version of feudalism. If we could never explain how such cardinal, qualitative changes take place, what they depend upon, what they are caused by, then we could not understand the life of man. Sociology could never become a science. To the Marxist, a sociology that is incapable of getting beyond a static framework would be an admission of defeat, an acknowledgment that the chief problems cannot be solved.

How does Marx try to solve these chief problems? He once put his basic approach to them into a nutshell. In a passage that has become famous, he wrote: ·

The general conclusion at which I arrived and which, once reached, continued to serve as the leading thread in my studies may be briefly summed up as follows: In the social production that men carry on they enter into definite relations that are indispensable and independent of their will; these relations of production correspond to a definite stage of development of their material powers of production. The sum total of these relations of production constitutes the economic structure of society—the real foundation, on which rise the legal and political superstructures and to which correspond definite forms of social consciousness. The mode of production in material life determines the general character of the social, political and spiritual processes of life. It is not the consciousness of men that determines their existence, but, on the contrary, their social existence determines their consciousness. At a certain stage of their development the material forces of production in society come into conflict with the existing relations of production, or—what is but a legal expression of the same thing—with the property relations within which they had been at work before. From forms of development of the forces of production these relations turn into their fetters. Then comes the period of social revolution. With the change of the economic foundation the immense superstructure is more or less rapidly transformed. In considering such transformations the distinction should always be made between the material transformation of the economic conditions of production, which can be determined with the precision of natural science, and the legal, political, religious, aesthetic, or philosophic —in short, ideological—forms in which men become conscious of this conflict and fight it out. Just as our opinion of an individual is not based on what he thinks of himself, so can we not judge such a period of transformation by its own consciousness; on the contrary, this consciousness must rather be explained

> from the contradictions of material life, from the
> existing conflict between the social forces of produc-
> tion and the relations of production. No social order
> ever disappears before all the productive forces for
> which there is room in it have been developed, and
> new, higher relations of production have matured in
> the womb of the old society.[1]

There is a good deal of meat in this closely packed
shell. In explaining society, Marx distinguishes first of all
between relations of production (or property relations)
and material powers (or forces) of production. The former are the legally sanctioned relationships in which individuals or groups can stand to one another in the
process of producing the necessities and luxuries of life.
In a slave society, we see the master-slave relationship; in
feudal society, the serf-lord relationship; in capitalist society, the employer-employee relationship. (Each of
these societies has of course many other legally sanctioned economic relationships; we have mentioned only
the principal ones.) The sum total of productive relations in a given society Marx calls the "economic structure" or "foundation" of that society.

The material powers or forces of production include
the natural sources used—such as land, mineral resources, and the like—as well as the particular tools, instruments, techniques, methods, and skills that have
been created, and the human labor power itself that
man possesses. Thus we already have two levels in the
process of production—the physical, technical level of
natural resources, tools, skills, and the interpersonal level
of relationships of authority, ownership, control.

There is a third important level in Marx's anatomy of
society, a level he calls "superstructures," that is, sys-

tems of law, government, religion, arts, philosophy, and the like. Social change—human history—takes place because of interrelationships among these three levels. What happens is that the built-in need of human beings to supply themselves with the goods necessary to survival and enjoyment creates a constant pressure for improvement of the forces and tools of production. Modifications in environmental conditions add to the causes of change in these matters. These technological changes force accommodating changes in the relations of production; and those changes, in a more subtle and less visible fashion, induce accommodating changes in law, politics, religion, arts, philosophy—that is, in culture generally. Such is the character of the inner dynamics of history, through which quantitative and qualitative changes in human society take place. As we see, Marx calls the qualitative transitions periods of "social revolution"; this becomes the basis of his whole theory of revolution, widely misunderstood, which we shall deal with later.

Marx uses the term "consciousness" (also "ideology") to designate such matters as legal systems, forms of government, religions, arts, philosophy. It is through these "superstructures," consciously formulated and taught, that man expresses the rules and principles he accepts, the image of himself that he has, the goals that he sets up. It might easily seem that it is just this consciousness that determines what happens at the economic foundations. However, Marx holds it is mainly the other way around: What happens at the economic base predominantly determines what emerges in the social superstructure. While the causal influence is reciprocal it is by no means equal.

In Marx's thinking, what is termed the "class struggle" is central both to the process whereby relations of
production determine social superstructures (social existence determines social consciousness), and to the
processes of change in the relations of production themselves (the whole drama of conflicts between new forces
of production and old relations of production). However, in order to understand the class struggle, and the
decisive role it plays, we must first understand clearly
what the Marxists mean by a class.

The key to this meaning is the economic character of
the standard used. That is, what the term "class" desig-
nates is a group that has a common relationship to the
means (forces, tools, techniques) of production, a relationship of such a nature as to bring the group into necessary economic conflict with another group that has a
different relationship to these same means. The common relationship that slaves have to the means of production is that they (the slaves) can be legally compelled to work upon them, although they do not own
them, and that they themselves are among the legally
negotiable forces of production owned by others. The
common relationship of slaveowners to the means of
production is of course that they own at least some of
them, and can sell them if they wish. The built-in conflict of interests is obvious. The slave wants to own himself and the fruits of his labor, while the master profits
from owning the slave and what the latter produces.
The struggles between these two classes, well known to
history, have often taken the form of physical revolts
and bloody reprisals.

Under capitalism, the chief classes in the productive
system are not slaves and slaveowners, but proletarians

(industrial wageworkers) and capitalists. The relationship of proletarians to the forces of production is that they work upon them for wages but do not own them (in a controlling sense), while capitalists own them, and thus realize profits (or a return in the form of dividends or interest), but do not necessarily work upon them.

We see again the built-in economic conflict. The greater the amount (or rather, percentage of what is taken in) that goes to the owners as profit, the smaller the percentage that can go to the workers as wages. Put differently, it is to the advantage of wageworkers to get higher salaries, while it is to the advantage of those who pay them to get a higher profit; at the same time, it is clear that both wages and profits must come from the same "pot." We are not saying that the *total amount* of the "pot" from which wages and profits must both come would be larger if the owner paid extremely low wages. Everyone knows that, if wages are lowered beyond a certain level, the productivity of workers decreases, thereby decreasing the total returns of the enterprise. The point is that, even when the workers are producing "normally," there still remains the question of raising or lowering the *share* that goes respectively to wages and to profits, within the limits that are compatible with the operation of "going concerns."

Marxism lays emphasis on the fact that the struggles between classes are not *essentially* psychological, or personal, or matters of individual outlook and choice, once the people involved are in process of economic interaction. Slaves can be "treated well," in the sense that prisoners in a jail can be treated well; but, so long as they remain slaves, deprived of liberty and of economic and civil rights, there remains also a deep-seated antagonism between the group of slaves on the one hand and the group of slaveowners on the other, an antagonism that can be eliminated only by eliminating the slave-master relationship itself.

Although the specific characteristics of the struggles between classes are obviously different under capitalism, the Marxist holds that the same point applies, in the sense that these struggles too are independent of the will of the persons involved, once the economic relationship has been entered into. The bargainings and negotiations between unions and management can be, and often are, carried on for long periods with politeness and observance of parliamentary ground rules. Of course, they also occasionally break out into physical violence, even including killings. But, however the conflict of interests may be handled, at whatever level the struggle is conducted, the conflict exists in the worker-employer relationship in a sense in which it would not exist, if the relationship were that of equal partners.

For example, if conditions become such that business declines, and a given firm would go bankrupt if it tried to continue paying wages to its present labor force, it is compelled to discharge a certain percentage of its workers. Appeals, made on grounds of sympathy, morality, or humanitarianism, that the workers in question should not be discharged would be quite irrelevant. In fact, if they were acted upon, the consequence might possibly be to make the situation worse, since bankruptcy would mean loss of employment for many more. In short, what is necessary for a firm to remain in business under capitalism is not that everyone should remain employed, but that the owners should make a profit. In a profit system, that necessity is beyond the control of the owners themselves.

We shall see later that the Marxist believes there is a socioeconomic arrangement under which it is possible to eliminate antagonistic class relationships of the kind we are discussing. But it is important to note that, even if they were inevitable under any social system whatsoever, and the Marxist was thus mistaken about the possibility of eliminating them, it would still be a fact that it is this type of antagonistic economic relationship which, in his terminology, is the defining standard of the classes he is talking about, and the genesis of what he calls "the class struggle."

It is also important to realize that, as these terms are defined in Marxism, class membership and class struggle are facts, whether recognized or not, in the same sense as a person's specific gravity is a fact, whether or not he thinks about it or understands it. That is, a person whose income consists of dividends from shares of stock he owns might never give thought to that fact, or conceivably might not even know what the companies in which he shares ownership actually do. What makes him a member of the capitalist class is not that he thinks of himself as such, but that the economic basis of his way of life is *profit*, which comes to him because he *owns* certain means of production. Just so, a worker on the assembly line of a factory is a member of the working class or proletariat, not so long as he thinks of himself in that way, but so long as the economic basis of his way of life is *wages*, which come to him because he *works* on certain means of production. (As we shall see presently, people who work for wages, but not on means of production, belong, strictly speaking, neither to the class of capitalists nor proletarians.) Put in Marxian terms, the chief point we have been here making can be summed up by saying that there is a distinction between class membership and class consciousness.

There is also a distinction between class consciousness and class loyalty. Marxism recognizes that it is fully possible for individuals consciously to work against the long-time interests of the class to which they economically belong. The best example of this is Engels himself, who was a manufacturer. Perhaps there are more numerous examples of the reverse—workers who psychologically and politically "identify" with the capitalist class. However, no matter who changes sides in his loyalties, the struggle remains so long as there is a conflict of interests.

Just as there are individual persons who belong partly to one class and partly to another (a factory worker, 5 percent of whose income is from stock dividends is, so to speak, one-twentieth a capitalist), so also, as we noted, there are groups who, strictly speaking, do not belong to any class. Service and professional personnel such as clerks, lawyers, teachers, doctors, engineers, and the like do not, as such, either own means of production or work directly on them to produce commodities. However, they become attached, in their functions (and loyalties), to one class or another which is concerned directly with the means of production. Though their economic status is in a sense less direct, Marxism recognizes that their importance can be very great, not only because of the contribution they make in relation to the productive process as a whole, but because of the part that they can and do take in class struggles.

We have used as examples only the chief class relationships in the selected society. Besides the classes that play leading roles, there are others also directly involved with the means of production, but whose relationships are in certain respects economically different from the leading ones. Under capitalism there are farm owners and farm laborers, landowners and sharecroppers, and various other groupings. But the decisive struggles—those that tell the main story of any society—are between the chief classes.

Marxism emphasizes that so long as economic class struggles take place, they are bound to have all sorts of manifestations, repercussions, and consequences, conscious and unconscious, at the superstructural level—the level of legal codes, forms of government, moral systems, religions, arts, and the like. It could hardly be otherwise, because what is at stake in the class struggle is of such basic importance to all human life. What is at stake is nothing less than control of the means of life, not only in terms of physical survival, but also in terms of opportunities for cultural development, training, growth of creativity, enrichment of personality, and the like. The whole way of life is in question; he who controls the means of life can control the way of life.

When the Marxist says that the legal code of a given society reflects the class struggles that take place in that society, and, in a partisan sense, reflects the interests of the ruling class, he is not pointing to anything covert, conspiratorial, or in the nature of a violation of the law. He is pointing to the content and character of the law itself. That is, the law itself in a slave society declares slavery to be not only legally permissible, but physically enforceable by the power of the state, if the slave tries to rebel or escape. Only someone who would wish to argue

that slavery is a relationship that is in principle equally
to the benefit of master and slave could maintain that
legal slavery represents human justice.

We shall examine later the Marxist's reasoning in relation to what he holds to be the partisan character of
the laws that are basic in capitalist states. What we have
already said about the legality of slavery is sufficient to
make clear what he means when he says that the class
struggle manifests itself in such a sphere as law. The
same thing applies to the whole matter of forms of government. It is obvious that not all groups and classes in
a society are equally powerful, in terms of their being
able to obtain and utilize the means of life, growth, and
development, and in terms of their chances of winning
out in the competition with others. It is also obvious
that it would be an extremely strange state of affairs
(which could not be expected to last for any great
length of time), if the form of government did not reflect the facts of power. A government by its nature has
responsibility and authority in respect to a whole range
of matters that affect the various needs and activities of
social groups. No social group or class could be dominant if the government were not of the type to meet its
needs and facilitate its activities. A slave society does not
have an anti-slavery government. The very meaning of
saying that a certain class is the dominant or ruling
group is that the government meets its requirements and
sanctions its powers.

The same situation must of course obtain at the
moral level. For example, the prevailing morality of a
slave society could not be expected to condemn slavery,
nor could the prevailing morality of a capitalist society
be expected to condemn private ownership of capital. It

is not an accident that the greatest philosophers of antiquity (including Plato and Aristotle) defended the principle of slavery, restricting their criticisms mainly to such contentions as that Greeks should not enslave fellow-Greeks (as Plato maintained in *The Republic*), or that some of the wrong persons were respectively masters and slaves (as Aristotle maintained in his *Politics*). Nor is it an accident that the greatest theologians of the Middle Ages, such as St. Thomas Aquinas, defended serfdom and monarchy. The very fact that the *sincerity* of these thinkers is not called into question makes the underlying situation all the more significant, as presumptive evidence of the strength of the influence that is exercised upon moral conceptions by the nature of the existing system of productive relations.

In religions, the very way God has been historically conceived of and referred to—as lord, master, king, and the like—bears the marks of relationship to dominant socioeconomic classes. More important, perhaps, is the fact that the same body of religious doctrine has been officially and predominantly interpreted in one period in a way that conforms to the power of the existing ruling class, and then interpreted in an opposite way in a different period when there is a different ruling class. When slavery, serfdom, and absolute monarchy were predominant socioeconomic institutions, the predominant interpretation given to Christianity by the existing churches was such that these institutions were compatible with it. After they were overthrown and new institutions took their place, the churches then predominantly took the view that the new institutions were compatible with Christian morality, while the old ones were not.

It is important to note, in this connection, that Marx-

ism does not deny that moral codes and religious doctrines can exercise an effective influence toward bringing·
about changes in the economic system of a given society,
even when these changes are not welcomed by the ruling
class. What Marxism maintains is that the chief causal
determination runs in the other direction—the economic system, and the changes taking place in it, influencing changes in moral conceptions and religious interpretations. In other words, the causal process is two-way,
as between economic foundation and social superstructure, but the two ways are far from being equal in
strength.

Such are the concepts that are basic to the Marxist
explanation of human society in its process of
development: forces of production, relations of production, economic foundations, social superstructure, class,
and class struggle. In order to see these at work, as the
Marxist sees them in terms of his theory of historical materialism, let us take for illustration some basic aspects of
the historical transition from feudalism to industrial
capitalism. Why did that transition take place? What
are the chief causal factors to which it can be traced?

In order to answer these questions, the Marxist looks
first to the nature of the existing means (forces and
technics) of production, and the operative, legally sanctioned relations of production. He concentrates on how
they are working out, in respect to whatever needs and
problems of the society are growing more acute, more
pressing. What conflicts are present? What changes are
taking place? What is growing stronger, and what
weaker?

The economic system of feudalism is of course chiefly
agricultural; hence, the principal basis of production is

the land, together with tools and technics that are relatively simple. Processes of manufacture are not well developed or highly efficient. Trade and commerce have not reached an advanced stage. At the same time, there is a growing population, and a steadily increasing demand for necessities and luxuries. There are also tales and reports of opportunities for acquiring gold and silver, and valuable commodities of various kinds, by trading with, or forcefully penetrating, distant but little known places, such as India and the East generally.

In order to exploit these opportunities, and to increase productivity in response to growing needs, there is a constant pressure to improve tools and methods of production, to voyage farther, to solve the scientific and technological problems that are connected with geography, navigation, metallurgy, and the like. It becomes clearer and clearer that there are great potential rewards and values in an increase of commerce, industry, and trade. At the same time, the ruling class of hereditary lords is not one whose functions or training are of the kind to equip it to meet such needs, or to take advantage of such opportunities.

The new wants and demands are best met by people associated with industry and trade—ship builders, manufacturers (master craftsmen), merchants, bankers (money lenders). These are the burghers, who make up what is later to be called the "bourgeoisie," or capitalist class. This whole group does not as yet have either the social prestige or the political power of the landed aristocracy; they are placed at a disadvantage by the law, as well as by tradition and custom. The laws of the feudal order not only grant all sorts of privileges to the nobles, which automatically place them in positions of power and authority; these laws also tie up and immobilize economically the land and its natural resources, through all sorts of hereditary and monopolistic restrictions (such as entail, primogeniture, and patents), which hamper or prevent industrial development.

What industrial development most needs is that restrictions shall be removed and possibilities of manufacture and trade opened up, so that it would be permissible, for example, to buy and sell desirable parcels of land and natural resources on the open market, to manufacture a large variety of goods, and to be able to transport them and sell them freely. What such development also needs is the possibility of attracting workers from one place to another, in response to new opportunities and the demands of new enterprises, and the possibility of employing and discharging them at will in accordance with changes in the conditions of demand, supply, and competition. But to accomplish these things, it was necessary to challenge and drastically to modify a whole complex of existing laws, which expressed the powers and privileges of the dominant class of hereditary, land-owning nobles. Put bluntly, it was necessary for the bourgeoisie to replace the landed aristocracy as the ruling class.

In emphasizing that this was what was actually done, the Marxist is not maintaining that the actors in the drama consciously put it to themselves in those terms, or that they planned out the process as a whole. They simply did what they felt to be necessary, in order to fulfill the needs and possibilities of their basic way of life. Not only did the relatively new, young, and growing bourgeoisie do just that, but the relatively old and established landed aristocracy did the same. This class naturally resented the increasing power of the industrial class, and resisted by every means its intrusion into the places of authority and dignity. The gigantic contest between these classes was not only fought out directly in such fields as law, government, and politics, in ways that included a good deal of physical strife, warfare, and revolution (the English, American, and French Revolutions of the seventeenth and eighteenth centuries played important parts in the story as a whole); it was necessarily fought out also, with varying degrees of consciousness in regard to its full implications, in the area of moral values, religious interpretation, and the arts.

What we have been saying amounts, of course, to but the briefest sketch of the factors involved in the historical transition from feudal society to modern industrial society. Yet it may be sufficient to indicate how the Marxist uses the central concepts of his historical materialist method. He concentrates on the big changes, and tries to explain them by tracing them to the actions of major social classes in their struggles for power, the decisive key to which is control of the means of production.

In this particular instance, we have spoken mainly of the role of two classes, each of which was, in its own way, a dominant and "exploiting" class. (The precise meaning that Marxism attaches to the term "exploitation" we shall examine later.) In this connection we should remember two things: First, the victory of the bourgeoisie over the feudal aristocracy was attained not by its own efforts alone. Each of these contending classes of course tried to rally to its side those in the classes lower down—peasants, serfs, and workers of all kinds, among whom there was much discontent, misery, and suffering. It is not unnatural that the bourgeoisie was more successful in these efforts than its rival, for the latter was the embodiment of the existing order, the visible master responsible for what had been happening. The bourgeoisie usually carried on its struggles, therefore, in the name of the whole people and of human rights generally. However, it is not difficult to see that the actual outcome of the contest was the establishment of a socioeconomic order that greatly favored the interests of the bourgeoisie over those of the lower classes. After the English Revolution of the seventeenth century, the masses of the poor were in fact almost as poor as ever. After the American Revolution, slavery was left standing as a legal institution. After the French Revolution "settled down," so to speak, it was not the majority who were in power, but the bourgeoisie. The majority, who were in the lower classes, made gains, all in all; but the minority, who constituted the upper class of capitalists, made much greater gains.

The second point that should be borne in mind has significance in relation not only to the specific transition from feudalism to capitalism, but to all such transitions. That is, it was possible for a relatively new and originally weaker social class to win a victory over the established ruling class, only because the movement of the basic economic and historical forces favored the new class by adding cumulatively to its strength, and by diminishing the strength of its opponent. Although such factors as the leadership, courage, and will of individuals is important, they are not decisive. The factors that are decisive are the large-scale conditions of man's environment and society, which develop through individuals, but in their cumulative effects go beyond the scope of any individual, however powerful.

Thus, in the transition we have been examining, the objective fact was that the power of the feudal ruling class had an agricultural base, and that this class, as a functioning whole, had no interest in or motive for developing industry. The fact that the continuance or even the improvement of agriculture could not solve the increasing problems of society, that these problems could be solved only by the development of industry, and that such a development was objectively possible rather than being illusory, meant that the hereditary nobles could not long remain the ruling class. The whole growth of science and technology continuously added strength to the industrial forces, as did the geographical discoveries and exploration that accompanied this growth.

In other words, while the landed aristocracy may not have known it, what they were fighting was not only the bourgeoisie, but history, science, and technology. Thus they were bound to lose in the end, and their opponent was bound to win in the end; it was only a question of how long it would take. Of course, in the long run, any victor may be superseded in his turn; but that does not change the fact that at a given time one side is growing stronger and the other weaker, nor does it change the great importance of knowing which is which. Also, this dynamic of history does not determine in advance that all future transitions must inevitably be accompanied by the kind of violence and slaughter that have characterized transitions in past history. There is no reason in principle why knowledge of the objective facts of social evolution should not give man the power to foresee that certain outcomes are the inescapable consequence of the cumulative trend of events, and to realize that violence is not a means of resisting the irresistible.

In this connection, it is important to understand clearly Marxism's conception of the "inevitability" of historical outcomes, such as the victory of the capitalist class and the defeat of the feudal aristocracy. The certainty of the latter's defeat was not exactly analogous to that of a swimmer whose strength grows weaker while the tide runs heavier against him, for the tide is in no way the product of human action. A more accurate analogy would be the certainty of defeat for a group knowing only the use of the crossbow, and trying to hold out in a castle besieged by another group, who are not only growing in numbers, but who are finding it increasingly profitable to make and use firearms of increasing destructiveness. The defeat in this instance is inevitable not *apart* from what any people do, but precisely *because* of what people do because they are people.

In other words, the fact that history has certain inevitable outcomes does not *ipso facto* make it a "fatalistic" process, since this inevitability is seen not as something imposed upon man by an external force, but as the result of the very human activities that he pursues consciously and intelligently. This is determinism in the sense of a rationally understandable causation, in the light of the fact that man has needs and capacities, the interaction of which makes it necessary for him to do certain predictable things when he is faced with certain situations. But this is not fatalism, for the latter maintains that a specific result is going to come about (a) whether man does anything or not, and (b) no matter what it is that he does, if in fact he does anything.

For this reason the Marxist holds there is no warrant for the charge sometimes brought against him that he is guilty of inconsistency in that, on the one hand, he exhorts the workers to organize, to form a strong party, to engage in political struggles, and to be ready to make sacrifices for the triumph of their cause, yet on the other hand simultaneously tells them that their victory is inevitable. If their victory is inevitable, why do the workers need to struggle and sacrifice? Or, to put it the other way, if they need to struggle and sacrifice, how can it be consistently said that their victory is in fact inevitable?

The answer to these questions is perhaps best seen in terms of the role of prediction. When a physician says to a patient: "Your recovery is certain; take this medicine and follow my directions," he is making a prediction. Like every rational (as distinguished from fatalistic or mystical) prediction, it is made in the light of the laws and the conditons that are operative in the situation. That is, the physician is reckoning on the fact that the patient wishes to go on living, and will follow the directions given. The physician may be factually mistaken about the laws and the conditions, but there is no logical inconsistency between his directions and his overall prediction. That is, if a certain patient did not really wish to live (hence, did not take the medicine, nor follow directions), there was a factual error in the premises from which the prediction was made, but no inconsistency in the reasoning as a whole. The Marxist's reasoning is that, given the basic conditions and laws relating to human behavior and social forces, people who are suffering will seek a way out of their suffering, that their reason will show them that some ways are more effective than others, that they will exhort one another to do everything that is possible, and that those ways which fit in best with the underlying movement of the decisive forces will succeed.

While this point applies in general to historical predictions made by Marxism, its specific content has to do with the predicted breakdown of capitalism, about which we have not yet spoken in any systematic way. Since this issue is so important a part of historical materialism, let us examine in some detail the thesis that the Marxists present in this regard, and the evidence they adduce to support it.

Put bluntly, the thesis is that, while capitalism represents a necessary, progressive, and socially valuable step beyond feudalism, it also goes through an evolution; and reaches a point at which it can no longer solve the problems that have arisen, and must therefore give way to a system capable of doing so. What are these problems? As we might expect, they are rooted in dynamic interactions between a changing system of productive forces and a system of economic relations that becomes increasingly incapable of dealing effectively, in terms of commodity output and the needs of people, with the developments, the potentialities, and the problems involved.

The problem that the capitalist system did solve was how to increase productivity, how to build up industry and trade. It did this by creating an open market where there had previously been monopolies and restrictions of all kinds; by making the land and its resources negotiable commodities on the market, whereas previously these had been immobilized within static patterns of hereditary succession; by freeing the serfs from their feudal bonds (and the lords from their feudal obligations), so that the former group became a freely moving mass, whereas previously it had been hemmed in and tied down. In the course of time, not only did cities increasingly take on the character of industrial centers, and increasingly overshadow the countryside in economic importance, but the growing population of the cities became increasingly exposed to a type of insecurity and misery that was peculiar to the new system.

In fact, it might almost be said that massive economic insecurity (which is a quite different matter from a low standard of living) comes into the human picture for the first time. Although the economic productivity of the feudal system was fatally limited, there were no detached, independent masses of population "on their own," for whom the society had no prearranged place, for whom no one in authority was "responsible." However, the capitalist system, by its nature, gave rise to an increasing number of wageworkers, who were legally free to make their livelihood as they wished, in competition with one another for the jobs that were available. They were free to become capitalists if they could; they were also free to suffer in poverty and misery if no employer found it profitable to hire them.

By why should it come about that no employer would find it profitable to hire them? The answer to this question began to make itself felt as time went on; it became designated as the business cycle. That is, since production under capitalism necessarily aims at making a profit in a competitive market, the producers are in competition with one another. Each is free to produce whatever type of economic commodity he wishes (so long as it is legally salable on the market) in whatever quantity he believes he can sell, at whatever price he calculates to be most profitable. (We are here describing the "classic" conditions of the "free economy" in its earlier stages.) But it soon became evident that the Achilles heel of the whole arrangement was that, in these circumstances, the market becomes recurrently overproduced.

That is, where there is no overall planning of production, no coordination of total volume with the needs and capacities of the consumers, or, to put it differently, where production is geared to individual competition for private profit, it is inevitable that from time to time more goods will be thrown upon the market than the consumers are able to purchase. When this happens, workers must be laid off, since it would be foolish for their employers to have them go on producing goods for which there is no market. The disemployment of wage-workers further depresses purchasing power and, hence, further reduces sales, which, in turn, necessitates the disemployment of still more workers. Thus, while prices have plunged lower than ever, goods are less accessible than ever to those who need them most, because of widening unemployment and shrinking wages among those who are employed. A "free" economy, not subject to centralized, overall control, becomes subject to the impact of periodic "depressions," with all their disastrous consequences for the lives of the masses. The tragic effects—psychological, physical, cultural, and moral—of protracted involuntary unemployment, especially on the part of heads of families who are generally not possessed of any significant reserves of accumulated wealth, are too well known to need detailing here.

Another potent source of economic insecurity, of large-scale disemployment under the economic relationships inherent in capitalism, is seen in the invention of new machines, the creation of more efficient productive processes, the whole progress of technology. How could this be the case?

As the Marxist sees it, these socially unfortunate results come about, not because there is anything inherently bad or regrettable in inventing more powerful machines, more efficient methods and labor-saving devices
(quite the contrary), but solely because of the economic
relationships that are legal and dominant under capitalism. That is, when a more efficient machine is invented,
by means of which, for example, fifty workers can turn
out the same number of shoes in seven hours that previously required the labor of a hundred workers, the
owners of the shoe factory will naturally wish to utilize the new machines. They naturally reason that they
can thus cut down their outlay for wages, and thereby
raise the margin of profit, because the price of the new
machines will be less, over a period of time, than the
wages of the workers those machines are capable of re-
placing. (If this were not so, there would be no economic reason to use the machines; the important problem arises only from those cases where it is so.)

Although the owners thus feel that they have no cause
whatever to regret the advent of the new machines, but
rather, as owners, cause to rejoice, the workers will inevitably take a very different view, so long as they are dependent for their income on wages paid by an owner
who is competing for a private profit; the new machine
is a threat to their continuity of employment. Of course,
a certain number (but not all) of them might find employment in making the new machines. But this requires
retraining; it is a practical possibility for only a small
portion of the displaced group. Also, labor unions can
be counted upon to wage a bitter struggle to prevent
either the introduction of the new machines, or the dis-
placement of workers after their introduction. But they

can hardly be expected to be more than partially successful, if the machines really are in the nature of labor-saving devices, and the market remains a private and competitive one.

The Marxist points out that the more socially efficient and just way to meet the situation is obstructed under the conditions of capitalism. That is, it would be better to have the workers remain on the payroll producing the same number of shoes (or more, if desired), without loss of wages, though working fewer hours. But the owner cannot be expected to see this as good business. His advantage lies in greater profits, and the new machines create the opportunity to increase profits by reducing the amount of wages he must pay.

While Marxism, as is well known, takes its stand on the side of the workers, its solution of such a problem as this does not consist in trying to prevent the use of more efficient machines. Instead, its solution is to pass from the private ownership of all such means of production to collective ownership, from a profit base to a cooperative base, from unplanned to planned production. These are of course the conditions of socialism, a concept we shall examine more in detail in the following chapter. If the means of production are collectively owned, instead of being owned by one group seeking profits and worked by another dependent on the wages it receives from the first, then there will be no motive to throw workers into involuntary unemployment because of the invention of better machines. The advantages of the new machines can accrue to all; everyone can remain employed, at the same salary, and for fewer hours.

The same reasoning applies to the problem of over-production, the "business cycle," and the general unemployment that we discussed previously. That is, if the means of production are collectively owned, there is no reason for the production plans of the different factories, plants, and other such agencies to be kept independent of and secret from one another. Production can then be planned in the light of overall needs, potentialities of growth, and other relevant factors, in such a way as to preclude glutting the market or plunging the working population into mass involuntary unemployment. Any increased production—whether it be brought about through the invention of more efficient machines, the discovery of new resources, or the development of better methods of working with the present facilities—can be absorbed, without interrupting the continuity of employment of the labor force, or reducing its wages, because there would be no group whose advantage would be served by disemploying a portion of workers rather than shortening the working day for all.

Thus the basis of the Marxist analysis goes back to the pressures that are created by the evolution of the forces and methods of production. If improvements made at that level begin to be obstructed by the kind of economic relationships that are prevalent, that are legally permissible and enforceable, then a contest will inevitably take place between those who stand to gain and those who stand to lose from a continuance of the old system of economic relationships. Each class will in the main act in the light of its own interests, and in the end the victory will go to the class whose interest coincides with the fullest utilization of the increased powers emerging from the given means of production.

The Marxist would strongly emphasize what is implied in this last consideration, because at first glance one might be tempted, in relation to such a matter as technological improvement, to draw the conclusion that it is the capitalist class whose interests coincide with the utilization of the labor-saving machines, while the workers' interest is to prevent their use. But the Marxist holds that such an appraisal suffers from two defects: It looks at the situation statically, in terms of an artificially delimited short run, and it assumes the capitalist framework as a constant. But the point is that the capitalist's *way* of utilizing the new machines is one which is not compatible with the life needs of a larger group, the workers. This makes it socially inefficient and increasingly unviable. Of course, if there were no other way of utilizing the improved technology, save the capitalist way, the situation would have to be accepted as an unfortunate instance of a problem without a solution, a tragedy from which no exit is possible. But the Marxist points to another way, which he sees as coinciding more fully with the interests of all those who work: collective ownership, whereby improvement of machinery results in shorter hours for all, and loss of productive function or economic security for none, and under which there would be no motive to disemploy persons for the sake of profits, or to restrict productivity to keep prices high.

Although, as we have noted, the Marxist maintains that the basic dynamic of history is not moral feelings, but economic relationships, we can sense in what has been said how moral feelings are intertwined with these relationships, and play a part in the drama. This is also seen in the Marxist analysis of a category central to the capitalist system as a whole—that of profit, which, it is held, necessarily involves exploitation.

Profit must of course be distinguished from the return that an owner, executive, or manager receives for work done as a planner, administrator, director, or the like. Actual services of any kind are legally and normally recompensed by fees or salaries. Profit has no relationship to anything of that kind; it comes to an owner whether or not he does anything of that kind. That is, he may, if he wishes, pay others to do these things out of his profits, which come to him just because of the fact of ownership. Put differently, to be successful, within the standards of capitalism, a business must make a profit, over and above what it pays out to all who *work* for it in any way, and at whatever level (plus what it pays out for any other expenses). This profit is divided among the *owners*, in addition to any other compensation they may have already received for service of any kind to the business. From the technical standpoint the Marxist sees this as an unnecessary and disruptive drain on the productive process; from the moral standpoint he sees it as a form of exploitation. Why?

We have already examined the capitalist's position from the viewpoint of technical efficiency: When private owners compete with one another for a private profit, the economy as a whole is uncoordinated, unplanned, and disrupted by periodic crises of overproduction and underemployment. Moreover, there is no technical need for a class of owners apart from that of administrators, executives, and managers. Thus the Marxist holds that productive efficiency will be promoted by collectivizing ownership (a process that would normally involve legally determined compensation to previous owners), and then providing for individuals in the light of their services and needs. But there is also a moral aspect to the problem of profit.

That is, whatever a business sells can be created only by the labors, physical and mental, of human beings in relation to what nature provides. People, by working in some way, therefore add economic value to something when they make it into a commodity that is available to others for purchase. Suppose a worker thus produces some commodity, let us say a bench, in one day. Assume that his employer had to lay out, for all the raw materials necessary to make that one bench, and for all other expenses figured (save the worker's wage) in relation to the one bench, a total of $20. Assume that, when the bench is finished, it sells for $40. The worker by his labor has added an economic value in the amount of $20 to the materials. But, of course, he will not receive $20 as wages from the employer. If he did, there would be no profit for the latter. By the same token, if there is any profit for the employer (over and above what he is entitled to receive for any actual services he may have rendered as foreman, manager, or the like), that profit can only be the result of an act of exploitation. That is, the person who takes it rendered no actual service for it; he gets it by appropriating a portion of the value that has been created by others. This portion is what Marx called "surplus value," and the taking of it is what he saw as the built-in mechanism of capitalist exploitation.

In other words, after all socially necessary outlays have been made, capitalism necessitates a further outlay which Marxism sees as socially unnecessary and morally indefensible, the outlay that is known as a private profit. The transition to socialism and communism eliminates this, as we shall see in more detail in the following chapter.

QUESTIONS and REPLIES

1. *In* The Poverty of Historicism, *Karl Popper argues that the idea of an essentially historical social science, of a rational theory of history as a whole (one example of which is represented by historical materialism), is logically impossible. Popper sums up his reasons in five points, as follows:*

> 1. The course of human history is strongly influenced by the growth of human knowledge. (The truth of this premise must be admitted even by those who see in our ideas, including our scientific ideas, merely the by-products of *material* developments of some kind or other.)
> 2. We cannot predict, by rational or scientific methods, the future growth of our scientific knowledge. (This assertion can be logically proved, by considerations which are sketched below.)
> 3. We cannot, therefore, predict the future course of human history.
> 4. This means that we must reject the possibility of a *theoretical history*; that is to say, of a historical social science that would correspond to a *theoretical physics*. There can be no scientific theory of historical development serving as a basis for historical prediction.
> 5. The fundamental aim of historicist methods . . . is therefore misconceived; and historicism collapses.[2]

Popper adds: "The decisive step in this argument is statement (2). I think that it is convincing in itself: if there is such a thing as growing human knowledge, then we cannot anticipate today what we shall know only tomorrow." [3]

How does Marxism answer this argument?

As we have already seen, Marxism would have no objection to the first point, that is, that the course of human history is strongly influenced by the growth of human knowledge, although it does not consider this to be the *strongest* influence on the course of history. In any case, Popper's argument does not depend on this factor being the strongest; it is enough that it be acknowledged to be a significant factor and, since both sides do acknowledge that, the debate is not about the factual truth of a premise, but is essentially about what can be inferred from that premise. Popper holds, in effect, that in order to make broad predictions about the future course of history, one would have to be able to make predictions about the future growth of ideas, insofar as history is influenced by ideas. But, he argues, to predict future ideas would be the same thing as claiming to know today what we will actually be able to know only tomorrow, since these are future realities, not present ones. Hence, says Popper, there is no rational possibility of predicting the future course of history in the broad or overall sense, in the sense claimed by such thinkers as Marx, Hegel, or Comte.

The weakness in this argument is seen first of all in the vagueness of its terms. Popper is confusing the prediction that a certain idea will be proved in the future with the present possession of the data that are necessary to prove the idea. Suppose, for example, that on the basis of statistics concerning the relationship between past medical discoveries and the amount of research facilities and attention given to them on a national and international scale, a prediction is made about a future medical discovery, such as that the cause (or cure) of disease X will be found within twenty-five years. This prediction may in fact turn out to be either right or wrong; but, in order to make it, one need not claim to be in possession of the data that would *prove* the scientific correctness of the future discovery. If that were so, it would not in fact be a *future* discovery at all; it would be a present reality. To take another example, we can, on the basis of the accumulation of all sorts of evidence, predict that, within such and such a period of time, man will have mastered the difficulties and solved the problems that at present stand in the way of the human exploration of other planets. Again, this prediction may turn out to be either right or wrong. But it is clear that it can be made rationally now, on the basis of present evidence, in the same way as other empirical predictions must be made, without claiming to know now just *how* the difficulties will be mastered and the problems solved. There is a difference between predicting *that* an idea will be proved, and predicting *how* it will be proved.

It must also be borne in mind that, according to the theory of historical materialism, ideas do not influence history just by being discovered and logically proved. In order to influence history, they must be applied and utilized, and experience shows that they will be applied and utilized only when the actually existing social conditions (economic, legal, political, moral, religious) do not offer too great a degree of resistance to their acceptance. The fact that we can to a certain extent estimate differences of degree in such resistance facilitates the making of predictions about future ideas influencing the course of history.

2. *The capitalism of today is not the capitalism that*

Marx knew and wrote about in the middle of the nineteenth century. Today capitalism has accepted such developments as minimum wages, maximum prices, unemployment insurance, government regulations of all kinds, government operation (and even ownership) of railways and other transportation services, of power plants and other public utilities, of housing developments, and the like. Since capitalism itself has changed to such a degree, is it not necessary to conclude that Marx's judgments and predictions concerning the inability of capitalism to solve the problems that arise in the course of its development have become invalidated?

Marxists point out that all these changes are in the direction of socialism, and away from the "classic" characteristics of capitalism. Increasing social controls, increasing social services, increasing collectivization are quantitative changes within capitalism which foreshadow the nature of future qualitative changes that will result in full-scale socialism. Marxism has always predicted that capitalism would develop, through its own internal dynamics, more and more in the direction of a transition to socialism. Just as some problems of capitalism are solved to a small extent by these trends, so the major problems will be solved by proceeding further into socialism itself.

3. As new machines and other improved technics of production are developed under capitalism, would it not be possible for management to come to an agreement with trade unions to share the benefits in such a way that the present labor force is retained, with some reduction of hours but without reduction of salary, while the owners still obtain an increase in profits, although not as much as they would have if a portion of the labor force had been discharged, and the remainder had kept on working the same number of hours per week? In other words, could not capitalism absorb and benefit from new and improved technics, and at the same time avoid social dislocations?

The Marxist recognizes that a certain amount of such adjustment and compromise is always possible, just as it has always been in principle possible for employers to accept lower rates of profit in order to raise the wages of low-paid workers. But such tendencies are always relatively weak in practice, because they run counter to the basic dynamics of a profit-seeking system. Not only is this sort of thing, when it comes about, usually the result of bitter struggles, involving strikes and other disruptions of production, but even where some success is attained, it is but partial and temporary. As the Marxist sees it, the full potential of benefit, that is, the full saving of labor, in the sense of maximum reduction of working hours, can be brought about only where collective ownership eliminates the drain of private profit entirely.

4. Is not the private profit incentive necessary to insure that the best efforts will be put forward in the whole process of production, especially in regard to new and untried possibilities?

Marxism holds that such contentions rest on a basically faulty conception of human nature. People do not need the specific motivation of private profit in order to undertake important projects or to put forth bold and intensive effort, any more than they need the specific incentive of slaveowning. If private profit were absent,

other forms of power and prestige would operate as incentives, in addition to such incentives as creative challenge and moral feeling.

5. *Apart from the element of incentive, is not the in-
vesting capitalist entitled to profits (in addition to whatever compensation he receives in the form of fees or
salary for the performance of actual services as planner,
administrator, or the like), in view of the fact that he is
risking his capital?*

The Marxist's reply is that this might be a good argument if such risks were socially necessary. Since a different arrangement is possible (collective ownership of the
means of production), in which no private individual
would need to take an individual risk of that kind, there
is no justification for continuing to "reward" private individuals in this way, especially since the way happens to
pose a constant threat to the economic security of the
large group of wage earners, as well as to perpetuate the
supposed "necessity" of risk.

6. *Is there not, in addition, an ethical issue involved in
collectivization of the means of production, unless this is
done with the consent and agreement of the present private owners, the existing capitalist class?*

There is an ethical issue involved, but it has to be
judged in terms of the lasting welfare of society as a
whole, since this is a matter that directly affects the life
of everyone. In this connection, the Marxist's reasoning
is similar to that which underlies what is known as the
right of eminent domain, by which the government is
empowered to take over any piece of private property,
such as a dwelling or farm, and to pay the market price

for it (whether the owner wants to give it up or not), if it is necessary for some public project, such as a highway. Marxism is not against the principle of compensation, but recognizes that the old ruling class often resists physically, and that civil war sweeps away the possibilities of peaceful settlement and financial arrangements.

7. What is the relation between historical materialism and the science of sociology?

The Marxist claim is that historical materialism represents the only genuinely scientific basis for sociology. Earlier objections on the part of Marxists to the use of the term "sociology" (as having "bourgeois" connotations) have largely disappeared. Auguste Comte, the father of sociology, whose work established the term, was an older contemporary of Marx and Engels. His sociology, like Marx's, was essentially historical; but, unlike Marx's, it took its point of departure from the proposition that opinion rules the world; that, as men think, so they live; that the social institutions they set up in any period are the result of the ideas that are dominant in that period. The key to the social history of man therefore lies in the evolution of his ideas, according to Comte; and the best way to change society is to change man's ideas. This is what Marxists call an "idealistic approach." A materialistic approach, as we have seen, holds that it is mainly the other way around: As men live, so they think; ideas reflect their conditions and institutions, and also the struggles, contradictions, and problems that are inherent in the changes and development of the material conditions. When those conditions have changed sufficiently, then men change their institutions and also their general ways of thinking. In other words, historical materialism provides a foundation for sociology that is different from the traditional one.

8. *Is historical materialism an "ideology"?*

Yes. But that does not mean that it must therefore be false or unscientific. All social theories are called "ideologies," in the sense that whatever actual problems they select for study, and whatever actual conclusions they arrive at, have an effect, one way or another, on the class struggles taking place at the given time. Truth is objective; but the interests of different classes at different times have differing relationships to that truth.

9. *Is historical materialism a partisan sociology? Does not Marxism assert belief in what the Russians call* partiinost' *("partyness," partisan character or attitude)?*

The answer is yes, to both parts of this question. But again, the partisanship in question is neither a denial of the objectivity of truth, nor is it a justification of calling untruth truth. What, then, is it? It begins with the selection of problems, which in turn reflects, consciously or unconsciously, a certain system of values. A book on "Corruption in the Catholic Church" or one on "The Crimes of the Jews" might conceivably be accurate in all its specific respects; yet we know that dealing with that selected problem (especially in certain social environments) will have partisan consequences, and might possibly make more difficult the actual solution of the social problems dealt with. The Marxist feels that anyone who is not aware of such potential consequences is dangerously naive; on the other hand, whoever tries to close his eyes to them is simply trying to be neutral in a situation in which neutrality is impossible. The Marxist sees his partisanship toward the working class as based on the fact that this class has the strongest interest in getting rid of all classes, the strongest motive for doing those things that people must do, in order that society as a whole may evolve to a higher level.

4.

The Nature of Progress:
Revolution, Politics, and
the Future of Society

Long before Marx and Marxism, revolutions of course played a significant role in history, and were the subject of serious discussion in philosophy. They were numerous in the ancient world and in the Middle Ages. Aristotle devoted several chapters of the fifth book of his *Politics* to a detailed analysis of the causes and significance of revolutions, and in the twelfth chapter he entered into a critique of Plato's treatment of them. The "classic" English, American, and French Revolutions of the seventeenth and eighteenth centuries are recognized as focal points of culminating importance in the transition from the medieval world to modern times. When Marx characterized revolutions as "the locomotives of history,"[1] his statement was first of all a summation of past developments. There is no debate about whether revolutions have had an important role in history. The only debate is about their causes and their justifiability.

Marx, as we have seen, traces historically significant revolutions to the dynamics of interaction between the forces of production and the relations of production. Let us recall one portion of a passage that we previously quoted:

At a certain stage of their development the material forces of production in society come into conflict with the existing relations of production, or—what is but a legal expression for the same thing—with the property relations within which they had been at work before. From forms of development of the forces of production these relations turn into their fetters. Then comes the period of social revolution.[2]

This does not mean that every revolution which has taken place, every attempt to overthrow an existing government, must necessarily have arisen out of this deep-rooted cause. What it means is: (a) this deep-rooted cause does bring about a revolution (violent or nonviolent); (b) a revolution, to be of major sociohistorical significance, must spring from such a cause; and (c) the revolutions on which Marxism counts in the transitions from capitalism to socialism and communism must spring from such a cause. Force and violence are not *necessary* parts of the Marxist concept of revolution. Under certain historical and political conditions, which we shall presently examine in detail, a revolution could occur peacefully. However, it is recognized by Marxism that most revolutions have in fact involved physical, armed conflict, and that this contingency must be taken into account in dealing with the present and the future.

The essence of historically significant revolution is not just a change in personnel in the governing apparatus, or the fact that the government is modified, or pressured by a show of force on the part of groups of citizens into redressing their grievances. The former may be mere "palace *coups*," and the latter popular insurrections of limited aims and local character. The essence of significant revolution is that it brings about qualitative changes in the economic structure.

Three of the larger aspects of the Marxist concept of revolution emerge from what has been said so far:

1. Violence is not the main point, nor is it a necessary condition.

2. Attempts to overthrow an existing government, whether by forcible or nonforcible means, cannot be regarded in themselves as either good or bad, as either signs of social health or of social sickness. It all depends on the concrete conditions and problems.

3. Revolutions in the sense of radical or qualitative changes in the socioeconomic order are an inherent and inevitable part of the historical process. History without revolutionary changes would bear little resemblance to actual human history; it would encompass only quantitative, but not qualitative changes, and could look forward only to a succession of small-scale advances, but not to large-scale progress.

The question that usually occupies the center of the stage in discussions of revolution in general, and Marxist or Communist revolution in particular, is the issue of force and violence. What position does Marxist doctrine take on this question? As a point of doctrine, the position is neither unusual nor is it difficult to define. The fact that it is so ill understood in popular discussions is no doubt due to the large role that is played by emotional factors in such discussions. While these factors are in themselves understandable, they can obstruct understanding if they are allowed to dominate the situation.

Perhaps the most concrete way to express the doctrinal position is to say that it is essentially the same as that set forth in the *Declaration of Independence* by Thomas Jefferson and in works of English writers such as John Locke (e.g., the second of his *Two Treatises of Government*, Chapter XIX), from whom Jefferson derived it. (The fact that we find this position also in Marx is of course no accident, since he was a close student of, and much influenced by, the revolutionary thinkers of the seventeenth and eighteenth centuries.) In other words, the doctrine in question, usually termed the "right of revolution," was not original with the Marxists, although the Marxists added certain factors to it.

What it asserts is that forcible overthrow of government is justified when two conditions are simultaneously present: (*a*) when the existing government will not carry out the will of the people, the majority, in important matters, that is, when it violates their basic rights, and thus becomes a tyranny or despotism, and (*b*) when the people, the majority, feel this situation to be an unjust oppression, and support the taking of forcible measures against the government. These are what the Marxists later called the "objective conditions" of the revolutionary situation, that is, the situation that must obtain before violent revolution is justified. To these the Marxists, especially Lenin, added a third precondition, called "subjective": that there must also be present in the given situation, on the side of the people, political organization of sufficient strength, with leadership of sufficient competence to promise the successful carrying out of the revolutionary action.

It is perhaps important to emphasize that the predominant weight and content of Marxist philosophy is explicitly against the undertaking of any violent revolution which is opposed by the majority, and which is not likely to enlist the support of the masses. In other words,

there must be convincing evidence that the majority are
in support of so drastic a step, and that they are prepared to face the dangers involved in their active cooperation in carrying it out. Beginning with Marx and Engels, a continuous polemic has been carried on against
what is known as "putschism" (from the German word
putsch, "insurrection"), that is, the tendency to engage
in frequent and indiscriminate acts of violent rebellion
against the government, irrespective of whether the majority, the masses, feel themselves to be involved in the
issues, and are willing to support and take part in the
actions.

On a number of occasions prior to the Bolshevik Revolution of 1917, Lenin, as the leader of his group, rejected the proposals and arguments of others that a call
for an armed uprising should be issued, basing his refusal on the ground that there was not yet evidence that
the majority was in support of such action and would
give its cooperation. In an important speech delivered
on May 7, 1917, just six months before the outbreak of
the revolution, Lenin said: "The proletarian party
would be guilty of the most grievous error if it shaped its
policy on the basis of subjective desires where organization is required. We cannot assert that the majority is
with us. . . ." [3] Only later did Lenin feel that there
was evidence of majority support, which he then specifically adduced.[4] In another passage, Lenin says: "If a
revolutionary party has not a majority among the front
ranks of the revolutionary classes and in the country
generally, there can be no question of insurrection." [5]

This attitude on the part of the Marxists should occasion no surprise, as of course their movement is a mass-
oriented one, geared to the problems and activities of

the lower, most numerous classes. A very different attitude toward the majority is seen in such movements as Nazism and Fascism, which have an explicitly aristocratic orientation, an openly expressed contempt for "numbers" [6] (Mussolini), for the "democratic mass idea" [7] (Hitler).

At the same time there are, of course, great practical difficulties relative to proving, in any revolutionary situation, Communist or non-Communist, that violent action has or has not the support of the majority. When things reach a point where such action is seriously at issue, it is very seldom if ever possible to take an orderly and trustworthy ballot. To put it bluntly, the people no longer trust the government; and the government regards its most determined opponents as criminals. Where formal voting by the whole people is not possible, the majority will must be gauged in other ways. Such was the situation, for example, in the American and French Revolutions. In any case, the doctrinal principle, as such, is important, whatever the practical problems of implementing it may be.

The conditions under which the Marxist considers that a peaceful or legal revolution can take place are implied in the foregoing discussion. That is, wherever there is a democratic or parliamentary tradition, or a democratic process strong enough to implement the will of the majority, if and when that will is for so radical a change as that from capitalism to socialism, there is no need or justification for measures of force and violence. In 1872, Marx singled out Britain and the United States as countries "in which the workers may hope to secure their ends by peaceful means." [8] In 1874, he cited Holland as also being in this category.[9] In 1886, Engels restated his position, in his preface to the first English translation of Marx's *Capital*.

Of course, conditions of this kind are not static, and must be judged differently at different times. Later on, Lenin held that, though Marx and Engels had been right for their day about countries like the United States and Great Britain, a peaceful transition was not possible in them during the first two decades of the twentieth century. From the end of World War II up to the present, most Marxist leaders have held that where the majority will is for a transition to socialism, a peaceful change is once again possible, on the ground that the number and strength of governments today in "the camp of socialism" is so great that capitalist powers would hesitate to invite a contest of force by denying the will of the people.

In like fashion, the concept of "world revolution," in the "classic" sense of a more or less simultaneous transition from capitalism to socialism in the most advanced industrial countries of the world, has undergone modification. Again, it is held that, while the facts as they had developed up to Marx's day justified the original conception, the world-wide imperialistic manifestation of capitalism, which took place after Marx, altered the picture. The fact that the first large-scale and successful Marxist revolution took place in such an industrially backward country as the Russia of 1917, and that this was not followed at the time by revolutions in other major countries, necessitated the working out of new conceptions. Thus arose the doctrine that revolutions will occur in the "weakest links" of the world chain of imperialism, and that socialism can be built up in separate countries, one by one.

Marxist philosophers hold that such modifications of doctrine do not represent an abandonment of Marxist principles. Since Marxism stresses a dialectical outlook, it does not expect to remain static; and since it bases itself on scientific method, it is concerned with going where the facts lead. Doctrinal modifications of this kind are distinguished from "revisionism," which signifies the abandonment of theoretical positions in the absence of sufficient objective evidence.

The specifically political philosophy of Marxism is worked out in terms of doctrines concerning democracy, dictatorship, the state, law, parties, freedom, and the like. In approaching them, perhaps the main things to bear in mind are that, in consonance with the dialectical methodology, these doctrines are developed in historical relativity to changing conditions, and that the meaning of key terms such as democracy and dictatorship is not necessarily the same as that which prevails in capitalist culture.

Let us begin with democracy. In the capitalist or bourgeois tradition, democracy is associated with such factors as a multiparty system, parliamentary balloting, the legal possibility of an organized political "opposition," along with freedom of speech and associated civil liberties. Essentially, it is construed as a method of making political decisions, rather than in terms of the kind of decisions made. It is thought of chiefly as a principle applicable to politics and government, rather than as a broad social principle which should manifest itself in all major institutions and in the cultural system generally. In contradistinction, the Marxist concept of democracy emphasizes goals rather than methods, and works itself out in relation to society as a whole, especially the economic system, rather than to a predominantly political context, in the narrower sense.

To put it bluntly, the Marxist's conception is that economic interests dominate politics and that hence professions of concern for the welfare of the majority must be implemented first of all at the economic level, else they will be at best unrealistic, at worst, hypocritical. But, it may be asked, if there is freedom of speech, a multiparty system, and majority voting, is there not full opportunity for the majority to obtain whatever they desire in regard to economic institutions, or any other institutions or laws? In other words, what objection does the Marxist have to what he calls the capitalist or bourgeois conception of democracy?

He feels it is superficial, because it does not take due account of the role of economic power. He reasons as follows: When freedom of speech results in any threat felt to be serious in relation to the economic foundations of the existing order, repressive legislation is enacted to protect these foundations from "subversion." Moreover, political power in practice becomes dependent upon the possession of economic resources. The fact that big electoral victories require big parties and big campaigns, and that these in turn require vast sums of money, almost amounts to a guarantee that parties openly opposed to the interests of big money are not going to get very far, and that the candidates of those leading parties that do have a chance to win are not likely to differ on economic fundamentals.

The Marxist considers it to be inevitable that, in a functioning capitalist society, the great predominant weight of popular propaganda (press, radio, television, and the like), as well as of formal educational influence, will be on the side of the capitalist system. In other words, a general contest of social ideas, in which every idea has an equal opportunity to present its case, is hardly conceivable on any large or significant scale, and difficult enough to attain even on a small scale, in special contexts of limited political significance. Only to the extent that the capitalist system breaks down or falters as an economic system does there come into existence the operative possibility of effective propaganda and of significant political activity directed toward supplanting the system. Until that point is reached (and reaching it is not chiefly dependent on political activity or propaganda of any kind, but upon the changing relationships between the forces and relations of production), the parliamentary and political contests and the norms of civil liberties will operate only within bounds that do not threaten the continuation of capitalism.

It is perhaps clear from our previous discussion how the Marxist judges the capitalist economic system in terms of the standard of democracy. While he feels that this system was a significant step ahead, in comparison with feudalism (in giving the people increased opportunities of development), it was not a system geared to the welfare of the whole people or even of the great majority. Its net effect, in a sense, was to make the ruling and exploiting class a somewhat larger minority than before.

As the Marxist sees it, what remains basically undemocratic about the capitalist system, that is, what cannot be remedied without a transition to socialism, is that the majority can hope to have economic security and continuity of employment (hence also the basis for a sufficiency of educational and cultural opportunities for their development as human beings), only to the extent that their work is a source of profit to the minority group of effective owners and employers. To put the matter more broadly, capitalism not only operates on the basis of an antagonistic class division, as between one group that works on the means of production but does not own them, and another group that owns them but does not necessarily work on them; it is the minority class that has the superior and privileged position.

The Marxist therefore feels that a serious and realistic concern for the welfare of the majority must be oriented toward making a transition from the private ownership of the means of production to their collective ownership. This is the only practical basis for getting rid of antagonistic class divisions, for assuring economic security for all, maintaining continuity of employment at the level of qualifications, and providing full educational opportunities at every level, as a social service without individual payment. Only under such conditions would it be possible to speak of genuine or operative equality of opportunity, of democracy as functioning in relation to the whole people.

These conditions are among the chief features of socialism, as that term is construed by the Marxist. It is clear to him that a system of that kind, once built, will be far more democratic, in the overall sense, than capitalism. However, to build it is no easy matter. Determined resistance may be expected not only from the capitalist groups that have suffered defeat within the country in question, but from capitalist classes in other countries, who cannot help being aware of the implicit threat to their own continuity of power. Under these conditions, the reasoning of the Marxist is in a sense quite simple: It is a greater contribution to democracy to build socialism, even if civil liberties must, to a considerable extent, be sacrificed for a period of time, than to allow the building of it to be delayed or jeopardized by party conflicts.

Expressed differently, until socialism is built, the government and party concerned with building it will represent primarily the class interests of the working class contending against a partially defeated capitalist class. Its contribution to democracy will consist, during this period, not in adhering to parliamentary norms, but in consolidating its victory, in order to be able to move to the establishment of new norms. Here, the reasoning is similar to that of a capitalist democratic government, during a war that threatens its existence: It is more important to democracy to suspend civil liberties for the duration, if that is necessary to win the war, than to jeopardize the chance for victory by adhering to the democratic norms.

When the Marxists call the government that thus undertakes the construction of socialism a "dictatorship of the working class," it is necessary to understand the meaning they attach to the term "dictatorship." In Western usage, especially in the ideological vocabulary of Nazism and Fascism, dictatorship implies a rejection of democracy in principle. As we have seen, this is not the case with Marxism, which considers every state a dictatorship to the extent that it uses instruments and agencies of physical force such as jails, police, armed personnel, and the like, on an organized, institutional basis, in order to handle problems and to deal with people. Such methods, though legal, represent physical dictation, the application of physical force sanctioned by law. As we shall note presently, Marxism envisages a future in which the state, in that sense, will disappear.

But so long as states in that sense do exist, the difference between them is not that some are dictatorships and some not; the difference is determined by the class interest that is predominantly enforced in this way, that is, by what class interest is embodied in the law that is physically enforced. Since socialism is considered to represent and reflect the interests of the working class—a majority—and capitalism the interests of the capitalist class—a minority—it is held that socialist democracy is on a higher level than capitalist democracy, even though both remain dictatorships, insofar as they deal with class conflicts by physical enforcement, each in its own way.

While some aspects of the Marxian theory of the state have been implicit in our discussion so far, let us now examine the conception as a whole, in the light of its central importance in political philosophy. On this question, as on others, Marxism takes an historical approach, and notes that the state, in the specific sense of a political institution that possesses a permanently organized apparatus of physical enforcement (police, jails, etc.), which it is empowered to use against the citizens themselves, did not always exist in human society. It made its appearance, generally speaking, in the transition from what is usually called "primitive communal society" to slave society.

The significance of this historical context is emphasized in relation to a number of factors. In pre-slave society, the members of the group have a common and communal relationship to the basic means of production —the land, fisheries, animals, fruit-bearing trees, and the like. Tools of production are as yet very simple, and available to all. Neither barter nor division of labor has progressed to any significant degree, save perhaps as based on sex; yet no group of women are negotiable slaves, as groups of both men and women will later become. Generally speaking, every man is an all-around man—producer, warrior, councillor—and would not willingly give up any of these functions, each of which carries status. Food, and the materials needed to make clothing and housing, are gathered or produced in common, and distributed in common. So long as this system obtains, there is no motive powerful enough to lead to the introduction of slavery; there is not enough for a slave to do that a free man would wish to hand over to him.

However, slavery becomes profitable when enough changes have taken place in the sources and tools of production to result in division of labor, and in the possibility of surpluses, which become objects of trade. Once the potentialities of these developments become plain, it also becomes plain that it would be desirable to keep slaves as private property, and to seize and hold other sources and means of production as private property. But these new relations of production, which create antagonistic class divisions—slaves and slaveowners, owners who do not work and workers who do not own—cannot be stabilized except by a permanent, specially organized apparatus of physical enforcement and a body of law defining crimes of property.

Thus the political state is born along with class divisions and private property in the means of production. What is distinctive about this institution is not such functions as planning, administering, or controlling.

These can be and in many areas of activity are carried out through institutional agencies other than the state. But the physical enforcement of law, especially concerning property, by a permanently organized apparatus, is a function unique to the political state. Thus the essence of the state is not administration as such, or even lawmaking, but the legally organized and empowered use of physical force against members of the society.

This is what will "wither away," or "die out," as Engels put it in *Anti-Dühring,* after communism becomes world-wide. It is argued that, just as the need for an apparatus of physical enforcement was originally called forth by the emergence of antagonistic class divisions in terms of private property in the means of production, so, when society is once again freed from such class divisions and such private property, the need for such an enforcement apparatus will gradually die out. People will then be better educated, better developed morally and emotionally (they will not be unavoidably forced, by the nature of the economic structure, into exploitative or destructively competitive relationships, either as perpetrators, or as sufferers), and they will learn to live according to rational rules, without the need of criminal laws enforced by an armed, specialized organization. When problems are handled with scientific competence, physical force becomes less and less necessary.

This position, as Marxism recognizes, implies a great degree of confidence in the potentialities of human nature. While it is clear enough that human society could claim to be operating on a much higher moral level than it is at present, if it were able to manage its affairs without the armed policeman, the penal institution, and the military establishment, there is of course great debate as to whether this higher level will in fact ever be possible. Marxism holds that its view is not grounded in a subjective utopianism, but in a sober estimate of the basic causes of crime, and of the potentialities of growth in such sciences as education, pediatrics, psychology, and sociology. Further aspects of this view will emerge in our further discussion of the nature of socialism and communism.

Let us examine the different sides of the concept of socialism, as it is understood in Marxism. Its basis is economic—collectivization of the means of production, thereby eliminating antagonistic economic classes, and creating the possibility of planned production and continuity of employment for all at the level of their qualifications. However, the principle of private ownership remains, so far as consumer goods are concerned—food, clothing, individual dwellings, furniture, pleasure vehicles, books, art objects, jewelry, personal equipment, and the like. Money is used, and wages are paid in accordance with the quantity and quality of work done.

A general principle of socialism is expressed in the formula: From each according to his ability, to each according to work performed. The Marxist maintains that capitalism could not claim that it has implemented either part of this principle. As regards the first part, capitalism has never been able to get rid of the business cycle, which entails periodic, mass involuntary unemployment. Insofar as such a phenomenon exists, people are prevented from working productively in accordance with their abilities. As regards the second part, it is the Marxist's contention, as we have seen, that private profits which go to private owners, not for productive work but for "risking their capital," are technically unnecessary, and prevent those who do productive work from receiving their full return, since the profit comes from their labor. Under collective ownership of the means of production, there is no private profit.

At the political level during the construction of socialism, as we have seen, there is a state with a form of government that implements the principle of socialist democracy, and that may be characterized as a dictatorship of the proletariat or working class. (Strictly speaking, "proletariat" means the industrial working class under capitalism; where socialism is being built, the term "proletariat" is usually replaced by "working class.") During the final stage of the construction of socialism in the U.S.S.R., Soviet leaders took the view that the functions and tasks of the state had changed to such an extent that it became more appropriate to refer to the government as a democracy of the whole people rather than as a dictatorship of the proletariat or working class, especially in view of the virtually complete elimination of internal class differences. What is involved in the state's new task—the task of effecting the transition to communism proper—we shall examine presently.

At the general cultural level, socialism involves a tremendous expansion of free social services, such as education and health care; special facilities for such groups as preschool children, the aged, the disabled, and expectant mothers; and exceptionally low prices for cultural goods (books, music, theatrical presentations, and the like). The Soviet Union, which represents the fullest development of socialism to date, has established an educational system that has been predominantly free of tuition payment at all levels, with provision for a stipend to students in higher institutions. Medical care of all kinds is likewise free. In consequence, Soviet health and education standards *in relation to the population as a whole* rose from the lowest European levels to the highest during the first twenty years after the revolution of 1917.

However, socialism as a whole is regarded as only one phase—the lower phase—of communism. Communism proper, in its full sense, is identified with the higher phase. There are great differences between socialism and communism proper, which it is important to understand. We are here speaking of the predominant currents of interpretation in the world Marxist movement, usually referred to as the "Communist" movement. There are of course other interpretations of the concept of socialism, which are connected with groups and parties that call themselves "Socialist" rather than "Communist," most of them also based on Marx's work. The terminology can thus cause confusion and misunderstanding, unless one keeps in mind the historical fact that Marx and Engels in their early period referred to their movement as "Communism" (e.g., *Communist Manifesto*), but in their later period used the term "Social Democracy," which became general. This was also the term used by Lenin in *his* early period. But the problems that arose within the movement at the time of World War I caused a split, as a result of which the more militant group (of which Lenin was an outstanding leader) revived the term "Communists," in order to distinguish themselves from the less militant, who continued to call themselves "Social Democrats," and their parties "Socialist" rather than "Communist."

How does communism proper, the higher phase of communism, differ from socialism? First, and most decisive, there is an economy of complete abundance. When the potentialities of new forces and technics of production, such as atomic energy, automation, and cybernetic systems, are not artificially restricted by the conditions of a private-profit competitive market, and the consequent threat of mass unemployment, it will become physically possible, even with a considerably reduced working day, to produce literally all the consumer goods that the population can actually use. After all, there is an operative limit to the number of chairs, tables, hats, pianos, cars, television receivers, radio sets, wrist watches, fur coats, pleasure boats, and the like that any one person can functionally utilize. There is no technical reason why that number, in relation to the entire human population, should not be reached and surpassed in the foreseeable future.

When the forces and instruments of production attain such a level of efficiency, and the relations of production are such as not to prevent their full utilization (that is, when they are collectively rather than privately owned), then it will become possible to acquire all commodities and services freely, without the condition of a money payment. In general, money will no longer be necessary. People who are capable of working will work the few hours per day that are necessary to meet all consumer needs, and the goods produced will be publicly available to all, as will all social services. (We are speaking here of necessary work. Most working activity is expected to be freely chosen and voluntary, at the level of professional and creative accomplishment.) The general principle of the higher phase of communism, or communism proper, as formulated by Marx in his *Critique of the Gotha Program*, is: From each according to his ability, to each according to his need. The concept of a wage payment that is based on the quantity and quality of work performed will thus be superseded.

The first reaction to this possibility of a superabundance of commodities and services freely available is usually that individuals will be tempted to take more cars, pianos, fur coats, or personal equipment than they can use, simply for the distinction of possessing a great deal. But the Marxist is counting on the fact that when the goods in question are really abundant and available to all, the feeling disappears that there is any desirable distinction in accumulating any quantity of them beyond what can be functionally utilized. Private possession of goods beyond the possibilities of normal use is a source of distinction, status, or power, only to the extent that there is an actual or potential shortage, relative to the population as a whole. In the absence of such shortages, it is held, money itself can and will become superfluous.

Since there will likewise be no shortage of physical and mental health care, or of educational opportunities and professional training, which are the prerequisites for creative growth, moral development, and the enrichment of personality, the use of physical force to try to solve problems of human relations will decrease, and the state, in the sense of an organized apparatus of physical enforcement, is expected, as we have seen, to "die out." However, it must be emphasized that this disappearance of the state is considered possible only when communism, with its economy of unrestricted abundance, has become world-wide. So long as communism should exist economically in but one country, or a few, the class conflicts that remain in dealings with the other still capitalist countries would preclude the abandonment of organized armed forces.

Thus the withering away of the state, under worldwide communism, does not mean the withering away of work, or planning, or administration, but only of the organized use of force against people. As we noted previously, this entire doctrine involves a conception of human nature, an image of man that rejects both the aristocratic view that the potentiality of higher development (in the sense of ability to benefit from higher education, to grow creatively) is by nature confined to a small minority, and the pessimistic view that man's essential nature is and forever will be sinful, physically combative, and oppressive toward his fellows. The Marxist conception of human nature is one that intends to make room for practically indefinite growth in moral quality, as well as in intellectual capacity and attainment.

Though these are views that one ordinarily calls "idealistic" rather than "materialistic," the latter term is used by the Marxist because he bases these views upon his estimate of the results of scientific findings. In fact, as we shall see in the following chapter, the Marxist feels that problems of value, including moral value, need not be separated in principle from problems of fact, but can be approached objectively in terms of scientific method.

Under the higher phase of communism, even if that phase, in its less than complete form, is confined to but one country, or a few, the fulfillment of certain social ideals and objectives that have been discussed since the early period of Marx and Engels is expected to become possible. This process of fulfillment begins under socialism, and is carried to completion during the construction of communism. One of its objectives is the "disalienation" of man; let us examine what is involved in it.

The term "alienation" sums up that condition of the human individual in which he feels that his work, his way of life, his institutional and cultural environment are divorced from him, not fulfilling him but betraying him, both by omission and commission. He feels deprived of values essential to his own selfhood. In the modern world, this phenomenon has manifold expressions at the level of psychological, moral, and esthetic consciousness, and it is dealt with extensively through a variety of approaches that represent many different schools of thought. The Marxist holds that the roots of the problem of alienation are economic, and that the problem therefore becomes solvable only when certain changes are made in man's relationship to his working activity, to the way in which he provides himself with the means of life and development, both physical and spiritual.

In other words, alienation in the modern world begins with the fact that the great majority of people are spending most of their lives, most of their strength and energy, doing paid work, the conditions, objectives, and very possibility of which are not only set by others, but are set primarily in the light of what is profitable to these others, who constitute a small group. So long as this situation obtains, a pervasive sense of alienation is bound to follow, a sense that man is not master in the house of his own life. The Marxist reasons that, when collective ownership of the means of production has replaced private ownership, when the employment of the many ceases to be dependent on its profitability to the few, when people can not only count on continuity of employment at the level of their qualifications, but are relieved of the fear of shortages or of deprivation of commodities, then the chief causes of the sense of alienation will have disappeared.

To put this differently, a psychological, moral, or religious approach to the problem of alienation, which does not acknowledge and assist in dealing with its economic roots, can at best achieve a temporary alleviation of symptoms, but not a cure or a prevention. This fact in turn can easily lead to the specious conclusion that the difficulty is after all rooted in "the very nature of man" (which is beyond redemption in this life), that man must therefore resign himself to his irrational nature, and, accepting the fact that this world is a tragedy, hope for a better fate in the next. In this regard, the contrasting Marxist attitude could be viewed historically as an acceptance of the Aristotelian image of man as a rational animal, as well as of the Baconian concept that knowledge is power, but without an acceptance of the conservative political limitations and static socioeconomic context given these ideas by the earlier thinkers.

Another social objective that is expected to find the possibility of fulfillment in communism proper is expressed as the elimination of antagonisms and socially destructive conflicts between town and country. Big cities, under the impact of the forces of private competition and the drive for profit, have grown up in a way that has overemphasized the concentration of population and the accumulation and use of machines, irrespective of their psychological, moral, and esthetic consequences. The city dweller becomes deprived of the benefits to his physical and emotional well-being and to his esthetic development that may be found in continuous and familiar contact with nature as an integral part of life experience. In like fashion, those whose life is in the countryside have become victims of uncontrolled economic forces, and suffer in terms of an inferior economic status, as well as in terms of inferior educational and professional facilities and opportunities. Marxism maintains that this imbalance can and will be fully corrected in carrying out the construction of communism.

Another imbalance of similar proportions, which developed along with the growth of the capitalist system, is that between mental and physical labor. People have become increasingly separated into one group that is occupied too greatly with physical tasks, and thus suffers in terms of mental growth and intellectual values, and another group that is too greatly occupied with intellectual and sedentary tasks, and thus suffers in terms of physical development and general health. The economics of communism and the increased leisure that it will provide are expected to render such conditions unnecessary, and to afford the possibility of establishing a healthy balance of these factors in the life of the individual.

The Soviet Union is the first country in which a time schedule has been worked out in relation to the construction of any of the features of the higher phase of communism. The Program of the Communist Party of the Soviet Union, as adopted at its 22nd Congress, October 31, 1961, devotes considerable attention to the problems of implementing the transition from socialism to communism proper in the Soviet Union, as the first country in which this transition has been considered possible. The estimate given is that

> The material and technical basis of communism will be built up by the *end of the second decade* (1971–80), ensuring an abundance of material and cultural values for the whole population; Soviet society will come close to a stage where it can introduce the principle of distribution according to needs. . . . Thus, *a communist society will in the main be built in the U.S.S.R.*[10]

As we have seen, the chief feature that will remain absent until communism exists on a world-wide basis is the withering away of the state.

An aspect of Marxist social philosophy that has assumed increasing importance since the coming to power of strong Communist regimes is its teaching on war and peace. This issue not only became of great moment to the world at large, but precipitated a crisis of decisive significance within the Communist movement itself, immediately after the Bolshevik Revolution in Russia succeeded in consolidating its power. The expectation then, in the light of classic Marxist doctrine, was that similar revolutions would break out more or less simultaneously in the leading countries, thus making the revolution and the transition from capitalism to socialism world-wide.

When this did not happen, the question presented itself: Should the Soviet Union use its resources and manpower to try to build up socialism in one country, even though it was surrounded by hostile capitalist states, or should it expend its energies chiefly in military directions, inciting armed revolutions in other countries, and relying on a strategy of large-scale military efforts? Generally speaking, Trotsky held that Soviet Russia was too backward a country to be able to succeed in building up socialism by itself, and therefore should rely mainly on the possibilities of world revolution and a military victory. Lenin, on the contrary, maintained that socialism *could* be built in Soviet Russia, weak and backward industrially though her inheritance from Tsarist Russia was, and encircled as she was by capitalist powers. The fact that this path was taken, and eventually led to the attainment of the objective, naturally had tremendous influence in the world Communist movement toward gaining acceptance of the idea that the building of socialism, and subsequently of most features of communism proper, was not dependent upon world revolution or upon large-scale military action.

Marxist philosophy is neither pacifist nor militarist in principle. It neither renounces war altogether, as Quakerism and the philosophy of Gandhi do, nor does it glorify war and see positive value in it per se, as Nazism and Fascism do. It holds that use of the instrumentality of warfare is justified if a people is attacked or tyrannically oppressed. The basis of this justification is the traditional rights of self-defense and of national liberation, which of course are not original with, or peculiar to, Marxism.

It would be a cardinal error to ascribe to such writers as Marx, Engels, and Lenin the kind of attitude toward war that was taught by such figures as Hitler and Mussolini. In the latter's *The Doctrine of Fascism*, an ideological document central to the movement he founded, Mussolini wrote:

> First of all, as regards the future development of mankind—and quite apart from all present political considerations—Fascism does not, generally speaking, believe in the possibility *or utility* of perpetual peace.

> *War alone* keys up all human energies to their maxi-
> mum tension, and sets the seal of nobility on . . .
> peoples.[11]

Hitler in his turn wrote in *Mein Kampf*:

> Mankind has grown strong in eternal struggles, and it
> will only perish through eternal peace.[12]

Marxism has never developed doctrines of this kind.
Even the present militant position of Chinese Marxism
does not represent a preference for war as such over
peace, nor does it include the thesis that war embodies a
higher ethical value than peace, nor that military warfare is eternal. Neither did Trotsky in his day ever advance such doctrines. In this connection, it is significant
to note that Mussolini maintained that the state, precisely as an embodiment of force, is necessarily eternal.
He wrote: "Fascism conceives of the state as an absolute.
. . . The forms in which States express themselves
may change, but the necessity for such forms is eternal.
. . . The fascist state is an embodied will to power
and government: the Roman tradition is here an ideal of
force in action." [13]

Since World War II, a good deal of emphasis and
discussion have been given to the concept of the peaceful coexistence of states that have different socioeconomic systems, the peaceful coexistence of capitalist
states and those governed by Communist regimes. The
predominant Marxist view, the most influential expression of which has come from the Soviet Union, is that
such coexistence is at least possible, and that its possibility is strengthened by the growing power of the states in
"the socialist camp." It is clear from the content and
tone of contemporary sources, and from the general

teaching materials in current use in the educational systems of countries where Marxists are in power, that they firmly believe that socialism and communism can win out in any peaceful competition with capitalism. Thus the premise of their position is that they themselves have no desire to make the contest a bloody and destructive one. As we have seen, they feel that history is moving in their direction, that its movement is such that capitalism is growing increasingly weaker on a world scale, while socialism and the possibility of its development into full communism are growing increasingly stronger.

At the same time, it is stressed that the question of whether the competition between capitalist and Marxist states can be kept on a peaceful basis does not depend on the positions and policies of one side only. Both sides must have the will to keep the competition peaceful, and each side must accept the other as having equal rights with itself.

It is significant to note that, as events have actually developed in relation to ideologies, two conditions, when present, exercise a negative influence on the chances for peace: when it is held as a principle that all-out war between the conflicting ideologies is inescapable; and when it is believed by one side that the other side actually maintains this principle, in spite of anything the other side may say. This latter situation, although it is one in which the blame is shifted to the other side for the belief that war is inescapable, results in policies that contribute to making war inescapable, whether or not the other side does in fact maintain this principle.

The difference that has developed between the Chinese and Soviet Marxists in relation to peaceful coexistence appears to be not about whether war or peace is to be preferred, nor about whether either of these states should or should not initiate war upon other countries because they are capitalist, but about whether the United States, as the leading capitalist power, will inevitably take the initiative in forcing a military contest. The issue is not about the desirability, but the possibility, of peaceful coexistence on a basis of equal rights, with the major capitalist power of the present day.

Contemporary Marxists emphasize that peaceful coexistence is a concept that applies to interrelations among states. When they also emphasize that this concept is not intended to apply to the contest of ideas, of ideological principles, they do not, of course, mean that such a contest should become a military one. Their position is that the international contest of ideas should continue, that it is neither possible nor desirable to stop such a contest. However, a sharp distinction is drawn between the contest of ideas and the cold war, on the grounds that the latter is not in the nature of a debate about the theory and practice of social principles, carried on by the use of argument and counterargument, but is more in the nature of a feud carried on by the use of policies of nonrecognition, refusal to trade, denial of equal rights, and the like. The position taken is that the cold war can and should be ended.[14]

It will help to understand both the Marxist's concept of communism and his interpretation of freedom if we take into account the fact that he regards the higher phase of communism as that stage in the social growth of man that, for the first time, makes genuine human freedom possible, makes it possible for human life to move from the area of "necessity" to that of freedom.

However, it is emphasized that this cannot be done by denying necessity, that is, by denying that things happen in terms of cause-effect relations and general patterns of law. It can only be done by discovering what the cause-effect relations and the general laws are, and then using them in the interests of man, to free man from unhealthy forms of toil, and from oppression, so that he may grow to his full stature in every sense—the intellectual, the emotional, the creative.

Engels expressed this position in a statement which has become classic, but which has given rise to considerable puzzlement and misunderstanding, partly because its blunt and paradoxical form invites quotation out of context, and partly because of the continuing effect of an unfortunate translation. His original German reads: ". . . ist die Freiheit die Einsicht in die Notwendigkeit." [15] This is usually translated as "Freedom is the recognition of necessity," [16] or, "Freedom is the appreciation of necessity." [17] The more literal translation of the German word Engels uses (*Einsicht*) would be "insight," which actually conveys his point much better than either "recognition" or "appreciation." In the work in which this passage occurs, Engels is discussing science, and his point is that it is scientific insight—verified knowledge of causes and laws—that enables man to free himself from things that are harmful to him, and gives him freedom to do those things that are beneficial to him.

This thought was not original with Engels or Marx. In fact, Engels himself specifically traces it to Hegel; he might have traced it even further back, to Spinoza, Bacon, and others. What is specifically Marxian, and not shared by these earlier thinkers, is the extent to which this conception of freedom is worked out in social terms, that is, in terms of the thorough reconstruction of social institutions that is considered necessary in order to implement it in relation to the whole people.

QUESTIONS and REPLIES

1. *If national balloting is impossible in a revolutionary situation, how would Communists know whether or not forcible measures have the support of a majority of the people?*

The reliance has to be on such factors as observation of the temper and behavior of the people, what they are saying and doing; what happens in organizations of wide membership, such as trade unions; the degree to which local forms of protest are on the increase, and the like. This is, of course, a problem not only for Communist revolutions; it applies to pre-Communist, non-Communist and anti-Communist revolutions as well. For example, no trustworthy national ballot was cast, or could have been cast, on the question of launching the American or French Revolution. What took place was a series of meetings (in defiance of the existing government) attended predominantly by anti-government representatives from different parts of the country, who reported, deliberated, debated—and decided. If decisions of this kind are taken in error, that is, if forcible measures do not have the support of the majority, the revolution is likely to fail.

2. *Is it proper, in this connection, to adduce conditions of the eighteenth century, such as those of the American or French Revolution? In countries with a modern parliamentary structure, what need is there to invoke a "right of revolution"?*

There is need only to the extent that it is possible for the existing parliamentary structure to be, or become, incapable of implementing the will of the majority. There are of course many causes that might bring such a condition about—various forms of corruption, weakness, or tyranny.

3. *How is the large-scale bloodshed of a Communist revolution justified, such as that which took place in Russia?*

In the same way that the large-scale bloodshed of the American or French Revolution is justified; that is, it is argued that in the given circumstances the bloodshed is not the fault of the rebelling people, but of the government which obstructs the will of the majority. The majority in that case have only the choice between suffering indefinitely the oppression and bloodshed involved in a continuance of the old order, and risking the bloodshed involved in trying to overthrow that order so that a better one may be set up.

4. *Is it not true that the socialism which, it is claimed, has been constructed (e.g., in the Soviet Union) has not really eliminated oppressing classes, but has simply given rise to a new oppressing class—that of party bureaucrats and others who hold the positions of authority and control? What is the Marxist answer to this kind of charge,*

which has been presented, for example, by Milovan Djilas in his book, The New Class?

The answer is that it is possible, under socialism, for corruption of one kind or another to arise in the administrative apparatus, and for party bureaucrats, and others in high position, to become opportunistic, greedy, selfish, lustful for power, and so on, in ways that victimize and oppress people with less authority. However, two points are emphasized in this connection. The first is that this is *possible* under socialism, but is not *necessitated* by socialism. An analogy under capitalism would be running a factory dishonestly by paying workers less than the agreed wage or getting from them more hours of work than the agreed number. This is possible under capitalism, but it is not necessary, since a capitalist factory can be run without such cheating. The Marxist argument against capitalism is not based on the existence of illegal practices of that kind. It is based on allegedly oppressive practices and unjust relationships that are *necessitated* by capitalism, and which are legal under capitalism. To stay in business within the capitalist order, a factory must make profit; in the Marxist analysis, as we have seen, there is no way of making profit except by exploiting others, in the sense that the value which constitutes the profit is taken from those who work to produce it by those who do not work to produce the specific value that they thus appropriate.

Profit-making as a condition of survival in business demands that production be cut down when profits cannot be made (even though there may be great *need* for the commodities), which in turn means that workers must be disemployed, even though this may have very

destructive consequences for them, psychologically, edu-
cationally, and morally. These inherently antagonistic
relationships to the means of production create what the
Marxist calls "classes." These conditions are defects
which, he points out, cannot be eliminated except by
eliminating capitalism itself as a system. Other defects,
such as cheating workers out of the agreed pay, could be
eliminated without eliminating capitalism. In the same
sense, bureaucratic corruption and abuse of authority
can be eliminated from socialism; they are not necessitated by socialism itself, nor are they legal under it.

Moreover, it is important to note that the group complained of in this connection—party bureaucrats and
highly placed administrators—do not form a new economic *class*. To form a new class, they would have to
divide themselves off from those lower in the economic
scale by a differing (and mutually antagonistic) relationship to the means of production, such as owning
them, while others did not, with the consequence of
being able to live well (legally) without working, while
the others had to work. As it is, they are divided from
these others, not by a differing relationship to the means
of production (which are collectively owned), but by a
differing degree of authority. Unless the existence of
differing degrees of authority and of differing rates of
pay is in itself to be accounted an evil, then the problem
in question is of a different character from that which
arises from the nature of capitalism, and does not represent a condemnation of the system as such.

5. *What is the attitude of Marxism toward differing
rates of pay?*

It is basically the same as that toward differing prices

of goods on the market. So long as the economy is one that includes wages, prices, and therefore the use of money (as socialism does), the normal reason, economically speaking, why a typewriter costs $100 and an alarm clock $10 is that, all things considered, it takes ten times more labor time (at a like level of skill) to obtain the necessary materials and produce the typewriter. In like fashion, differing rates of pay should be determined by the differing amounts of training time normally required to reach the point of being able to perform the tasks in question. That is, if it takes five times as long to train an engineer as to train a carpenter, the engineer's salary should be five times as great. Marxists acknowledge that this principle is very difficult to apply, that there are many unsolved problems in connection with it, and that there have been many inadequacies in practice, under the conditions of constructing socialism. They also point out, as we have seen, that in the higher phase of communism, money is expected to disappear, since consumer's goods will be freely abundant, and therefore the problem of differential wages or prices would cease to exist.

6. *Does not experience (such as that of Stalinism in the Soviet Union) show that the attempt to build socialism and communism places too much power in the hands of the party, producing if not a new economic class, then a new form of tyranny, which should not be called a "dictatorship of the working class," but a "dictatorship of the party over the working class"?*

It is necessary to separate the problem of concentration of power from the problem of abuse of power. Marxism does not hold that power in itself is bad, any more than strength is in itself bad. Power can be abused, and undue concentration of power can promote its abuse. This is what happened in the latter portion of Stalin's career. Power was unduly concentrated, and oppressively used, contrary to law. This was not a phenomenon of the party as such, but of individuals, and the mistake of promoting the cult of an individual leader. Again, the mistakes and crimes involved were not necessitated by socialism as such or by a political party as such.

7. *What answer can Marxism give to criticisms such as those made in George Orwell's* Animal Farm *and* 1984, *and Aldous Huxley's* Brave New World?

One must first pin down precisely what it is that is being criticized in such books. In *Animal Farm*, for example, is it human nature as such? Is it all social systems, old and new, or just the socialist-communist system? Is it revolution in general, or just the socialist-communist revolution? If it is all these things in general, the old as well as the new (as often seems to be the case in the course of the story), then the answer is that this sort of criticism, if it is to be taken seriously, represents an oversimplification. Surely not all systems are equally bad, or just bad in general. It is necessary to distinguish among the problems of a given system, in order to determine which are solvable within the framework of that system and which cannot be solved except by a transition to a different system. However, the attitude that man is inherently incapable of improving his society at all would mean that deliberate social progress has never taken place, that man might as well have remained at the level of slave society or feudalism, that there was no gain in passing beyond either of them. The American

Revolution, then, was no gain; neither was the French Revolution, nor the English. It would have been just as well to go on with the feudal order. This is blanket pessimism, which cannot stand up under analysis. It is neither historically realistic nor constructive.

If, on the other hand, the satire and criticism are directed specifically against socialism and communism, with the implication that capitalism is a better system, which is free from the sort of faults depicted in the new social order of the "animal farm," or has faults that are less grave, then it can only be said that such a contention is not sustained by the story. To sustain it, the ordinary human farm would have to be as closely examined as the animal farm, and the two compared. As the story stands, the satire directed against the new system can give comfort only to those who assume that, when anything goes wrong with the new way, that fact constitutes proof that the old way was better.

In like fashion, one must ask: What is the thesis underlying 1984 and *Brave New World?* Is it that man *must* fail in all attempts to build a better social order? If so, the answer is that there is not sufficient evidence to make such a sweepingly negative judgment. If, however, such books are supposed to represent an indictment of Marxist conceptions only, the answer is that their approach is not a responsible one. What or who is accused, and exactly what is the accusation?

8. *To what extent does Marxism blueprint the content of the future social institutions that will exist under communism proper? For example, is it a point of doctrine that the family will be abolished?*

To deal with the latter point first, it is not laid down

that the family as such is to be abolished, but that the defects and negative aspects of family relations, which arose as a result of the distortions, imbalances, and deprivations of capitalism, can be abolished under communism. Marxists do not attempt, to any great extent, to predict or blueprint the detailed content of the social institutions of a distant future. A comment of Engels in his *The Origin of the Family, Private Property and the State* bears on this point:

> What we may anticipate about the adjustment of sexual relations after the impending downfall of capitalist production is mainly of a negative nature and mostly confined to elements that will disappear. But what will be added? That will be decided after a new generation has come to maturity: a race of men who never in their lives have had any occasion for buying with money or any other economic means of power the surrender of a woman; a race of women who have never had any occasion for surrendering to any man for any other reason but love, or for refusing to surrender to their lover from fear of economic consequences. Once such people are in the world, they will not give a moment's thought to what we today believe should be their course. They will follow their own practice and fashion their own public opinion about the individual practice of every person—only this and nothing more.[18]

In like spirit, Marx brushed aside criticisms that he failed to provide details of future social institutions, referring to such exercises as ". . . writing recipes (Comtist ones?) for the cook shops of the future." [19] Speculations or predictions about a distant future are of course to be distinguished from planning about the near future, which means taking responsibility for providing the means of reaching the goal aimed at.

9. *Does Marxism visualize communism proper, the higher phase of communism, as a final or culminating stage of social evolution, after which there will be no further important developments?*

Not at all. There are no prior limits of this kind to the possibilities of social evolution. However, Marxism does not claim at this point in human history to be able to predict what lies beyond the higher phase of communism. There are not enough data at present to make reliable predictions so far ahead.

10. *If evolution proceeds through the conflict of opposing forces, would not this mean that, if the conflict of social classes is eliminated, as it would be under full-scale, world-wide communism, then the evolution of society must come to a halt?*

No. It would only mean that the content of the conflicting forces, and the nature of the conflict, would change. While there would be no conflicts deriving from class antagonisms between groups of people, the limitless area of conflicts between man collectively and the forces of nature would remain, and be resolved at ever higher levels. It should be added that, according to Marxism, competition as such between people is not to be condemned; only its destructive or socially wasteful forms should be eliminated.

5.

The Nature of Values:
Ethics and Esthetics

Although this part of Marxist philosophy has been given least systematic development, among the traditional branches of the subject, its foundations are clearly marked out, and its relations with the rest of Marxism can be discerned. In this area, the basic philosophic problem arises from the fact that man is the kind of creature who not only says: This is so; That is different from this. He also says: This is *better* than that; This is good, and that is evil; This is beautiful, and that is ugly; and so on.

In other words, man cannot live, or at any rate does not, without expressing and applying value judgments. The most obvious manifestation of this fact is the universal existence of moral and legal codes which set up standards of right and wrong conduct, of permissible and impermissible action—standards that are imposed and enforced in many ways. There is no need to emphasize that these codes, and the way in which they operate, make a great difference in the lives of people, as do their standards, choices, and preferences as to what is beautiful or ugly, attractive, or unattractive.

Two sets of questions about all this—one factual and one valuational—have long engaged the efforts of philosophers: (1) How have these standards of moral value and esthetic value actually been arrived at? What have they been determined by? What do they depend on? (2) Since there is such a wide variety of standards, how can we discover the right ones?

The kind of answer that Marxism gives to these questions will be best understood by seeing it in the historical perspective of certain broad differences among influential traditional approaches. One such approach is that the whole thing is basically a matter of subjective, arbitrary taste. That is, there is no objectively correct way of answering such questions as, What is good? What is evil? What is beautiful? What is ugly? There is no way of proving that one answer is true and another false; it is a matter of feeling, and feelings differ. Therefore, each to his taste. Another approach, characteristic of institutionalized religion, is that moral values, standards of right and wrong conduct, are not created by man, but commanded by a supernatural deity. The standards are eternal and unchangeable; man must obey them because that is God's will. Disobedience incurs God's punishment, which may extend to an eternal life after death. A third approach is that man's values are neither subjectively arbitrary nor supernaturally commanded. Man himself creates his values; and the fact that he creates certain values and not others (or that one group holds certain values that another group rejects), is determined by causes that can be discovered and understood. The right values for man are determined by his nature—his needs and the potentialities he possesses for growth and development as a human being. Since these can be discovered by reason, objective proof as to the right values is possible.

Marxism rejects the first two approaches. It takes the third position, the basis of which it shares with various thinkers before and after its own appearance, such as Aristotle, Spinoza, Holbach, Comte, John Stuart Mill, Dewey, and others. While essential features of this approach are thus common to a number of thinkers, each gives it a different and distinctive development.

Let us first clarify the general basis of this approach, and then examine what was added to it by Marxism. The attitude or premise with which it begins might be put as follows. Man's past experience shows that he has solved many important problems by means of reason— by discovering causes and laws, preventives and cures, by using new knowledge to make predictions he was not able to make before, thus controlling outcomes in a way he could not before. Faced with the problem of how values originate, and which ones are right for man, there is no need to give up or to avoid this method of reason, at least until all possible efforts along that line shall have failed, or until the problem shall have been shown to be in some way inherently meaningless or absurd, like the problem of the color of square circles.

The Marxist view is that there is no evidence that the problem we are here concerned with is meaningless or absurd. No one can find or even define a square circle so as to indicate what he is talking about, but questions of value arise in our experience every day, and are decided one way or another every day. Should I go on with my present way of life? The answer is a value decision, and there is no such thing as not answering, since, even if I avoid answering in words or thought, I shall not be able to avoid answering in action or inaction. Likewise, there is certainly no warrant for saying that all possible efforts to deal rationally with these matters have already been made, and have failed. We are in fact in process of making such an effort, which should not be prejudged.

This effort proceeds from the fact that man can observe himself, can reason about himself, his nature, and his activities. When he does this, he readily takes in the fact that he is a social creature who lives in and through a network of relationships with other human beings. In such circumstances, rules of some kind must come into play. There is nothing mysterious about that. It is also plain to see that there are alternative sets of rules, and that changes might be made in any existing set. Therefore, the question of how any existing set of moral standards, or any existing legal code (or any operative set of esthetic norms) came into practice is in principle not different from any other broad historical question, such as how the concept and practice of democracy came into being. There are complexities and difficulties, but they are not a kind that precludes the use of observation, study, and reason. We are dealing with matters of fact, and the ascertaining of matters of fact.

But what about the problem of the right values for man, the problem of what choices he *should* make, not what choices he *does*, or *did*, make? Is that, too, a problem of fact and the ascertainment of fact, or does it take us into matters that cannot be handled by the rational methods proper to the handling of facts? The approach we are examining maintains that there is no unbridgeable gulf between problems of fact and problems of value, that the understanding of facts is the key to the solution of value problems. On what basis is this maintained?

The basis can be seen in the thought that what is

right for man depends on the kind of creature man is. In examining this thought, let us begin with what we all agree on, and try to follow out its implications. Food, health, and shelter are values to man. It is *better* to have these things than not to have them. But why? Clearly, because man is made in such a way, is composed of such elements, organs, and attributes that, in order to exist, survive, function, and develop as a man, he needs such things. At the same time, it is also clear that not all foods are equally good, or represent equal values, to all men. But do we not successfully meet this problem with the same approach? That is, by rational, scientific examination of the effects of a given substance on different types of persons, different age levels, different bodily states, and different living conditions, we determine what is good for whom. Certain nutritional substances are good for all; others for many; some for only a few. But even the goodness of those elements good for all humans is a goodness relative to the nature of *humans*; it is relative to the content and mode of operation of that set of factors that all humans have in common (and which, as a whole, *only* humans possess).

We are speaking at this point of simple and obvious values; but the same line of reasoning is applicable to all values. A moral or legal code is an attempt to select and define those actions and forms of behavior that are good and those that are evil, those that are allowable and those that are not allowable. If some particular form of behavior or action is being considered, is up for judgment, so to speak, there is no better criterion to decide whether it is good or bad than its effect on the possibilities of existence, survival, functioning, and development of humans.

In this approach there is implicit, as one can see, an acceptance of what might be called an "all-human standard," as distinguished from a standard that would decide questions only in the light of existence, survival, and development of some selected group of human beings. This acceptance, too, is considered to be determined by the objective fact that man is by nature a social or gregarious creature, who cannot exist, survive, or develop in the human sense, except as a functioning part of a human group. Thus, to the individual human, one of the greatest values is the existence of other humans. Only to the extent that objective evidence could be adduced to show that some particular group of human beings was completely devoid of any potential of value in relation to humanity, including themselves, would it be justifiable to exclude them from the human reckoning. But there never has been any such evidence, nor is it likely there ever will be.

In the light of these conditions, disputes about values, about whether this or that type of behavior is moral or immoral, for example, become amenable, at least in principle, to settlement by a finding of fact. In many cases, the facts may be difficult to find, as for instance, the facts about many diseases are difficult to find. But this kind of difficulty is very different from the logical impossibility of finding square circles or the theological impossibility of understanding the mind of God in the issuance of commands, or in the allocation of a certain fate to man.

Still, it will be asked, are we sure that we can prove objectively what is good for man in the ultimate moral sense? In matters of food and nutrition, we have an agreed and objective standard—the effect on physical

health, which can be checked and measured by various
forms of observation. But when we speak of such matters as certain creatures' existence, survival, functioning,
and development as human beings, does all this represent an agreed and objective standard that permits of
measurement in some way? The approach we are examining holds that it does.

In the first place, it is emphasized that there is a very
large measure of actual (if not always verbal) agreement
on basic values. In fact, do we not have practically universal agreement (at least approximately as near to complete agreement as we have in matters of nutrition)
that, other things being equal, pleasure is better than
pain, happiness better than misery, joy better than sorrow, health better than sickness, knowledge better than
ignorance, the possibility of growth and development of
one's organs and faculties better than the impossibility
of such growth and development, freedom of movement
better than arbitrary confinement? This list could certainly be lengthened. In any case, the main point is that
these value preferences are not arbitrary or temperamen-
tal choices. They are built into the human organism in
such a way as to demand recognition if the human organism is to function as such. They represent objective
facts about man, which afford the basis of a scientific
approach to ethics.

But suppose we are confronted by persons who make
statements such as the following: I am not prepared to
say that pleasure is better than pain, happiness better
than misery, joy better than sorrow, health better than
sickness. Perhaps, after all, pain, misery, sorrow, and
sickness represent higher values, and are better for us
than their opposites. Who is to say? I do not have to

accept these value judgments of others. They express only their tastes; mine may be different.

Probably our first reply would be: Are you sure that you do not in fact accept these value judgments which you say you are not prepared to accept? If actions speak louder than words as to what a person actually prefers—and they do—it will not be difficult to prove, in practically all cases, that the given person in his conduct from morning to night is seeking what he thinks will give him pleasure, happiness, joy, and health, rather than their opposites, other things being equal. (It is necessary to emphasize this qualification, "other things being equal," in order to be clear about the basis of choice. If a dentist says that he will leave it to me whether he is to use a painful or pleasurable drill on my tooth, that they are equally efficient for the job, then my choice is a clear one, with the "other things" being equal. If, however, he says the pleasurable drill will give relief for only a short while, whereas the other will provide lasting benefit, then the "other things" are not equal, and I might choose the pain now, but only because I am convinced there will be more health and pleasure in the long run.)

Still, there may be someone who in his very actions would show that in fact he does not prefer pleasure to pain, health to sickness, and so on. What then? We would then probably feel justified in treating such a person as abnormal, ill, or deranged, as one whose actions and judgments cannot be accepted as responsible, so long as he remains in his present condition. We would probably feel justified in saying that there have been causes in his life to make him seek to increase his pain and sorrow, ruin his health, and shorten his life, so that he has reached a point where he takes more satisfaction in seeking to do these things than in seeking to do anything else. But we are sure that, if these exceptional causes could be removed, the individual himself would agree that a greater degree of satisfaction, a higher happiness, is attainable in a life that is longer, healthier, and more joyful.

In other words, so long as the person remains in his abnormal condition, he is being told: Experience shows that the preferences you feel now result in less and less satisfaction, and less and less possibility of further satisfaction. They are in that sense false preferences, although we do not deny that you really feel them. You are not consciously lying; but you are deceived. Your feelings are adjusted to delusions rather than to realities, as these have been judged by the vast weight of evidence over the years, arrived at by the most fruitful and dependable methods mankind has been able to devise. This does not necessarily mean we will use physical force to make the individual conform to our standards (that depends on the specific forms his behavior takes); but it does mean we are rationally justified, by factual evidence, in drawing a line between sound and unsound value choices.

Must it not be acknowledged that this same type of situation may arise in any of the exact sciences, and that it is dealt with there in the same way? That is, if some few observers sincerely maintain that where all the others see something, they see nothing or see something different; or, contrariwise, where all the others see nothing, they see something (but have no confirmable evidence to support them), they must be told that, while their honesty is not in question, their vision is. The causes may be localized physiological ones, or they may relate to the general condition of their nervous systems.

In any case, when reports conflict, we must accept the one for which there is most evidence. If we are examining an area in order to ascertain what it contains, there is no way to decide what is really and objectively present in it save by accepting reports of human sensory perception, even though we know that certain reports can be mistaken. And there is no way to decide which are mistaken save by comparison, re-checking, and confirmation through further prediction. A minority can be right, but must prove itself so through evidence confirmable by others. In the same way, when we examine moral standards, we rely on knowledge based on the perceptions and feelings of human beings, even though we know that certain of these perceptions and feelings can be mistaken. What is objectively so, as distinguished from what is subjectively illusory, is determinable by basically the same rational methods in both cases.

What we have said so far about the general approach to ethics taken by Marxism does not represent anything original with or unique to Marxism. The spirit and basis of this approach, worked out in terms of differing historical contexts, may be found, as we have noted, in the ethical writings of such philosophers as Aristotle, Spinoza, Holbach, Mill, and others. Rejecting both the supernaturalistic framework in which moral values are seen as commanded by an omnipotent Deity, Who cannot be comprehended yet must be obeyed, and the subjectivistic framework which denies in principle that values can be proved in the same sense in which generalizations in physiology or history are proved, these thinkers confine themselves to human reason, and are convinced that values can be objectively verified.

Whatever strength this position has is not under-mined by the fact that the thinkers who hold it reach *differing* conclusions. The history of every field wherein a scientific or rational method has been used (astron-omy, physics, chemistry, biology, and so on) shows that different (and better) conclusions are reached from time to time, not because the method is capriciously or arbi-trarily changed, but, on the contrary, because the same method, persisted in, yields more and more accuracy in the reporting of facts, discloses deeper connections and relationships, and thus corrects previous shortcomings and errors. What is of primary significance is (*a*) the common ground shared by those who attempt to use the scientific method, and, (*b*) the profound difference be-tween this whole group, on the one side, and those who, on the other side, deny that a scientific approach is pos-sible in the given case, or who assert that there is a way to truth better than the way of science.

Let us now pose the question of what Marxism has added to this general approach (which has often been called "naturalistic," but which Marxism terms "materi-alistic"). In other words, what is distinctive or different about the conclusions reached by the Marxists on the basis of this approach as compared with those reached by others who have used it? Two factors stand out: the thorough reconstruction of social institutions, which, Marxism maintains, is a precondition of the practice and fulfillment of ethical values in the lives of the whole population, and the way in which Marxism accounts for past theory and practice in the area of values.

The first factor does not represent simply a stressing

of the conception that ethics is a *social* problem, a problem the solution of which is impossible except in systematic relationship to the specific nature of social institutions. Aristotle long ago gave massive emphasis to that conception, although its significance has often been obscured. We should bear in mind that Aristotle did not conceive of himself as writing two separate treatises, one on *Ethics* and another on *Politics* (which is the way we habitually publish these works). Rather, what he wrote represented to him one connected treatise (which he himself called, as a whole, *Politics*), the first part of which was an examination of what a good life is, and the second part an examination of what type of society, what system of social institutions, makes it possible for the good life to be lived. Aristotle shows the clearest possible realization (as Plato also does in, e.g., *The Republic*) that it would be unthinkable theoretically and unfruitful practically to deal with either of these matters in separation from the other. The reason is, as Aristotle put it, that man is by nature a political (social) animal. Thus the good life is necessarily a good social life; and a good social life necessarily implies a good society. In its full and positive sense, it is impossible to lead the good life except in the good society. Plato had already argued in the same way in his *Republic*, where Socrates points out that the just individual and the just life must be seen as functions of the just society. What is therefore needed above all is a description of what a just society would be; this becomes the central task of the dialogue.

However, the fatal limitation of the classic Greeks (and of the ancient world in general) lay in the irredeemably aristocratic conception of man which predominated. In terms of this conception, only a minority of human beings were considered to have the potentialities necessary to lead the good life, to attain true virtue. Only a minority were to be free citizens. Human slavery was maintained to be rational; it was justified on the ground that nature designs only a small group with sufficient rational capabilities to be able to absorb the education and training necessary to solve important problems of human life, and to take part in running the state. Nature designs others to be slaves, since they lack these capacities, but are fitted to do physical tasks and to develop manual skills. Aristotle held that such persons are necessary to a state, but are not really parts of a state; that is a dignity reserved to the citizens,[1] who constitute a kind of elite group.

In the light of these facts, what meaning did Aristotle himself attach to his doctrine that man is a social animal; that human virtue is developed reason; that the only path to sure happiness in a full life is the development and application of the powers of reason? It came to this: only humans can be rational, virtuous, and happy, but nature has designed humans so that only a minority of them have the potential necessary to the attainment of these ends. Man should design the state with these facts in mind as his starting point. He should not try to set up social institutions on the assumption that it is possible for everyone (or for the great majority) to develop to the point where they can absorb and benefit from higher education and complex intellectual training, where they can be trusted with the responsibility of running their own lives and taking part in decisions of the state. That would be a mistake ruinous both to the state and the individual. If we take that path, then even the few who are in fact potentially capable of attaining to higher reason, true virtue, and genuine happiness will probably be prevented from doing so.

Christianity, as it made its appearance in the ancient world, was of course in a significant sense a revolt against the aristocratic axioms. Its premises were that all human beings were children of God; that, as such, all were possessed of inherent dignity; that virtue was in principle attainable by all through obedience and faith, which could bring eternal happiness. These premises, however, contained a limitation of a different kind, in that the consummation and fulfillment of these values were not projected for this life and this world, but for an eternal life after death. Life in this world went on much as before: Such institutions as slavery, serfdom, divine right monarchy and hereditary nobility were sanctioned and justified by the predominant body of the Christian churches.

When political democracy made its appearance, it brought about changes in the political institutions that had dominated the feudal order; but the economic system (capitalism) that was coming to the fore along with the rising political democracy was not designed to bring into the lives of all the people the higher values it was capable of producing. The rules of its game were, it is true, different from those of the old order. However, the result was still a few rich and many poor; a few highly educated and many ignorant; a few fulfilled and many unfulfilled, even though in each respect the fortunate few were a larger minority than previously.

Marxism rejects the aristocratic image of man, not in the sense of denying that in each field of endeavor a small group will be found to excel the rest, but in the sense of denying that mankind is divided into masses on one side who are devoid of the potentialities of higher development in general, in all fields possessing intellectual, creative, or moral significance, and, on the other side, a small group who alone have these potentialities. It holds that the evidence at our disposal justifies the conclusion that all organically normal people (the vast majority) possess potentialities for higher development, although not all equally, nor in the same fields, and that improved methods of education and training will better bring out these potentialities, so that all people will be able to lead responsible, creative, fulfilled, and happy lives.

But Marxism does not believe these results can be brought about save on the basis of such a thorough revamping of the economic system as will make it possible to bring into existence that abundance of *operatively available* facilities and opportunities without which it is idle to talk of the higher development of all. Nor does it believe that this abundance can be brought into existence at any time or place, simply on the basis of desires, intentions, and moral enthusiasm. While these factors are necessary, they can bear the desired fruit only if the evolution of forces and methods of production has reached a point where the technical prerequisites are present. This is the combination of elements that is unique to Marxism in the history of ethical doctrines: the conception of the most thorough transformation of social institutions as the basis of man's moral fulfillment, and the conception that this transformation depends primarily on the development of the forces and methods of production. This position does not seek to deny the existence or belittle the importance of moral aspiration, moral feeling, brotherly love, and the like.

While insisting on their active role, it seeks to define realistically the conditions that determine the forms and the range within which these feelings and aspirations can find ever wider and stronger expression.

In regard to the second factor that distinguishes the Marxist approach to the field of ethics—the way in which it explains the past history of theory and practice in this field—we need only summarize certain aspects of our preceding discussions. The chief point is that, as regards the value patterns built into the existing institutions, in terms of the laws enforced by the power of the state, and the customs and mores enforced by the sanctions of public opinion, it is not predominantly a case of people first deciding what values they intend to fulfill, what moral standards and rules of conduct they hold to be highest, and then forming the economic, legal, political, and other social institutions, along those lines that will best implement the already chosen values. It is predominantly rather a case of those in control of producing the necessities and luxuries of life within some definite, concretely limited framework of technical and economic possibilities, pronouncing as moral, legal, and enforceable those ways of doing things, those rules of conduct and moral standards that, as they see it, fit in best with the nature of the productive system and their rulership of it.

It is important to note that these decisions have never in the past, at least since the emergence of classes, been taken by all people acting together on the basis of equal rights and powers, but on the initiative and through the predominant power of a certain group within the society. In other words, where there are classes with differing and conflicting relationships to the means of production, the moral standards, the rules and principles of conduct built into the existing institutions are those necessary to carry on the rule of the ruling class.

The morality thus built into and presupposed by the existing institutions of course finds its systematizers and defenders, its philosophers who give it a naturalistic or logical rationalization, and its priesthood who give it a supernaturalistic or religious framework. In a sense, the state always finds its church. Social existence predominantly determines social consciousness; the economic base predominantly determines the social superstructure. Hence, the functional patterns inherent in the operating institutions are usually defended both positively and negatively—positively, by justifying morally that which it is necessary to do, given the present framework; negatively, by sympathetically receiving protests against the evils, sufferings, and oppressions that result from the operation of the present system, by giving ceremonial expression to what might be called the "protest morality" that grows up within the existing system, at the same time teaching that the fulfillment of *this* morality is a matter for another life and another world. Meanwhile, people must accept the status quo, and obey the powers that be.

It is significant to note in this connection that Marxism sees an important relationship of the forces and means of production also to those new and higher, more inclusive, more benevolent moral principles, and those new visions of a better society that make their appearance within the old order. That is, such new principles and visions are seriously put forward, or at any rate are taken seriously and become influential, to the extent that they appear to be feasible in terms of some possible further development of the potentialities of the existing system of forces and relations of production, or in terms of new relations of production that would be feasible in the light of still further developments.

Marxism sees itself as sharing in this relativity in a conscious and rational way. As we have seen, the entire picture of socialism and communism, in its differences from the capitalist order, is, and is intended to be, highly charged with moral elements. All the new possibilities, the projected modifications of existing social institutions, are conceived of as those that will raise human life to a higher moral level, both by getting rid of old forms of evil, and attaining new forms of good. At the same time, it should also be noted that these new possibilities and modifications are projected specifically and systematically in the light of concrete factors in the evolution of productive forces and relations, and implemented by social planning in the light of the concrete overall situation.

In this picture of socialism and communism, sketched in the preceding chapter, we may discern the specific patterns of moral value that Marxism holds should be taken as goals now possible of implementation to a greater degree than ever before, if proper action is taken on a sufficient scale. Let us try to sum up these patterns and goals.

1. Full physical, mental, and emotional health of all the people.

2. Full education, professional training, and creative development of all people, to the limit of their capacities and desires.

3. On the basis of the foregoing factors, the enrichment and further growth of the individual personality.

4. The elimination of the economic exploitation of man by man, and of poverty in any form.

5. The elimination of destructive competitiveness, individual crime, and international warfare.

These are specific moral values that Marxism stresses at this stage in the development of mankind.

Let us turn now, at least briefly, to the question of esthetic values and the philosophy of art. Although, as we have remarked, this area of problems represents one of the less developed sides of Marxism, the basic features of the approach to it are clear. In the light of our foregoing discussion of what is meant by historical materialism, it will be understood that a materialist approach to art and esthetics, as conceived by the Marxist, does not in any sense represent a derogation of esthetic feelings and emotions, or a belittling of the importance of art in the life of man.

What this approach represents first of all is the effort to understand these feelings and emotions, and the whole role of art, in terms of natural and observable causes, rather than to assume that they derive from mystical, supernatural, or irrational sources, which would place them beyond the bounds of human comprehension.

If we pursue this analysis realistically, we see that the emergence of different art forms, trends, standards of beauty and of taste is in each case functionally related to the nature and content of the socioeconomic evolution that is always taking place, related to the concrete stage reached by this evolution. We see also, as a fact, that art, whether intentionally or not, always plays a role in relation to the great social contests that are taking place during any given phase of this evolution, in fields such as economics, politics, religion, and morals. Of course, there is a type of art that is designed simply to entertain and to amuse; but this is only one type of art, and it is difficult enough even for that type actually to remain neutral and amoral in its operative consequences. For what is in question here is not so much the subjective, conscious intentions, or lack of them, on the part of the artist, but the objective effects of his work in the lives of people and on the history of society. It is a fact that people see beauty in different things; but it is equally a fact that the different things in which they see beauty serve to create differential consequences, in relation to the whole range of social issues and the ongoing course of social evolution. Art, like morality, is a profoundly social phenomenon.

Marxists have usually characterized their approach to art and art criticism as social (or socialist) realism. As a doctrine, however, this does not exclude in principle many features of what we usually think of as romanticism, or even, in recent years, aspects of art that are associated with impressionistic and "modernistic" techniques. What it does exclude is a "photographic" realism or naturalism, which confines itself to detailed and mechanical reproduction of the surface of things or events, without communicating anything about the nature of those underlying currents that are working to bring about changes in the given subject matter. It also excludes the sort of romanticism, idealism, mysticism, or irrationalism that seeks to take account of deeper currents and relationships, but does so on the basis of weak or false premises. It likewise excludes that abstractionism which loses touch with objective realities, and thereby deprives itself of significance or meaning, other than that which is arbitrarily subjective.

What is central in social realism is the attitude or premise that art is all about life and the world in which man lives, and that the best art is that which takes due account (in its own esthetic way, of course) of the ascertainable truth about life and the world. If the art in question seeks simply to amuse or entertain, let it not do so in a way that at the same time raises false hopes or promotes false values. If the art has deeper purposes, then, whatever its techniques may be, it should do justice to objective truths, including those truths that can be confirmed at the moral level.

The questions of how much control should be exercised over art by the government or other official agencies, and what forms such control should take, are matters that are separate from the theory of art as such. They are also matters on which a wide range of difference has emerged among contemporary Marxists in different countries, and in the same country at different times. But, in whatever ways such questions are answered, either at the level of principle, or that of practice, it is clear that Marxists as a group reject such a premise as "art for art's sake" in favor of the idea of art for man's sake.

However, past discussions and debates about social realism[2] have made it clear that the Marxist approach in this respect is not to be construed as meaning that all art is to be condemned in which there is not an *intentional* and *explicit* relationship to morality and social progress. Neither is it to be construed as meaning that the productions of artists who themselves belonged to reactionary social classes must be judged negatively, or even that the works produced by artists who, apart from their art, took up a philosophical or political position condemned by Marxism as reaction, must therefore be of little or no value, as works of art. It is agreed that what is important is not the subjective intentions of the artist, or his class position by birth or background, but the actual content of his work in relation to the nature of reality and the course of social evolution.

QUESTIONS and REPLIES

1. Does Marxism hold the doctrine that the end justifies the means?

Not in any sense different from what we find in the prevailing moral theories and practices of other schools with which we are familiar. For example, the Judeo-Christian commandment says, "Thou shalt not kill"; yet throughout the Judeo-Christian world we find armies, navies, air forces, and police, all of whom have the legal right to kill under certain circumstances; and we find that the vast majority of churches do not teach that this situation is sinful, immoral, or a disobedience to the command of God. In other words, the position taken is that there are certain ends (whatever they may be—self-defense, protection of property, of personal rights, etc.) that do justify even so extreme a means as the taking of human life. This general attitude (that there are exceptional situations in which some rule of conduct normally accepted as morally binding may have to be violated in the interests of a greater good) is shared by Marxism. However, as we have seen, the basis of Marxist ethics is not supernaturalistic, as in the case of the religious tradition, but naturalistic.

2. *Is anything taken as an absolute in Marxist ethics, or is everything relative?*

What is taken as an absolute is the use of reason to discover what is good for man in the light of the facts concerning his nature, attributes, and potentialities, and to discover how the welfare of all can best be implemented in a specific situation. In the light of that absolute, the correct solution of concrete moral problems will necessarily vary with changes in the context and circumstances. The situation is similar to the problem of what is good for the health of people. The attainment of health, as determined by reason in the light of perceivable facts, is taken as an absolute. The use of reason reveals that specific prescriptions and norms must vary in accordance with the age, sex, past history, and present bodily conditions of the person under examination.

3. *Are spiritual values in any way recognized by Marxist ethics?*

The answer to this question depends on what is meant by "spiritual." If this term signifies the intellectual, the esthetic, or the moral (moral in the sense of the voluntary acceptance of obligations toward others, in the light of their welfare), the answer is yes. However, if by "spiritual" one means something deriving from a supernatural deity, or some other mystical source, the answer is no. As we have already seen, intellectual and esthetic values are rated very highly in Marxism; and the importance of moral obligation, deriving from the fact that man is a social or gregarious creature, is stressed.

4. Are "Christian values" rejected by Marxism?

Here again, the answer depends on what one associates with Christian values, considered as values, in distinction from the origin and source of the values in question. If one has in view simply such forms of behavior and feeling as brotherly love, charity, honesty, respect for the rights of others, and the like, then the answer is that Marxism does not reject these values, but stresses them, as we have seen. However, if one means to include in the idea of "Christian" an acceptance of the tenet that Christ is God, and that these values must be accepted on the ground that they represent commands of God, it is clear that Marxism, along with many other philosophical and religious systems, rejects that aspect of Christian belief.

5. Does Marxism believe in free will?

Once again, the answer depends on what one associates with the term in question. If one means by "free" that which is voluntary, which is the product of one's own wish, desire, preference, or choice when one is of responsible age and in possession of his senses, as distinguished from that which is the product of force or coercion imposed against one's will, then the answer is that Marxism does believe in free will. But if one identifies "free will" with wishes, desires, preferences, or choices that are not the product of natural causation, that are independent of past history, heredity, environment, bodily condition, education, and other such factors, then the answer is that Marxism does not believe in any will that is free from causation. Marxist philosophy argues that belief in a human will—a preference, wish, desire, or choice—that is free from natural causation is belief either in the proposition that something comes from nothing, or that something comes from something else, but in some magical way, outside and independent of cause-effect relations that are rationally confirmable. Marxism sees no reason to believe in either of these propositions; it sees no evidence in support of them.

6. Is freedom a positive value from the Marxist viewpoint?

It is, if due account is taken of whose freedom is in question, and of what the freedom is "freedom from" and what it is "freedom to." Freedom is never absolute, nor is it abstract; it is always relative and concrete. That is, if a certain freedom exercised by a small group (for example, the freedom of landlords to discriminate against tenants, or of employers to discriminate against candidates for employment, on grounds of religion or race) is destructive of the welfare of a large group, that particular freedom is not good, and must be curbed. Freedom *from* compulsory school instruction, or freedom *to* sell guns on the open market, are not necessarily positive values; they may be negative, harmful, depending on the concrete conditions and circumstances. In other words, not all restraints can be judged to be bad, nor all freedoms judged to be good.

Another way of putting the same point is to say that not all people need the same freedoms or the same restraints at the same time. It depends on their problems and surrounding circumstances. The Marxist regimes that have so far come to power are usually taken to task on the ground that they do not grant the kind of freedom of speech, press, and political activity, the kind of civil liberties, characteristic of democratic capitalist regimes. The reply is that the concrete problems and conditions in those countries that have so far been trying to replace capitalism with socialism as rapidly as possible, were and are such that it has so far been more important to free the masses of their people from illiteracy and ignorance, disease and early death, poverty and insecurity, than to extend the kind of political freedom and civil liberties that prevail under capitalist democracies. The reason advanced is that the most pressing problems of the populations involved were economic in their roots, and called for a thorough revision of the system of land ownership, industrial production, and employment. This involves huge undertakings, which can be carried through only on the basis of national planning and the cooperative effort of all over a considerable period of time. It is held that in the given circumstances, the attempt to set up the capitalist democratic system of political and civil liberties would jeopardize the success of these undertakings.

The critic of Marxist regimes usually identifies freedom with the absence of direct government interference; but the Marxist argues that whether such "freedom" is good or not depends on what the given government is trying to do and what the problems of the given people are. The press in capitalist countries is freer from control by the government or the political party in power than is the press in Communist countries; but the press in Communist countries is freer from the control of advertising or private wealth than is the press in capitalist countries. There is no "free press" in general, just as there is no "free world" in general. Freedoms are selective; they must be related to specific problems and needs.

7. *What is meant by "class morality"? According to Marxism, does each class have its own morality, and is each class right from its own point of view?*

What is usually meant by "class morality" is the principles, rules, and norms that are predominantly carried into practice by a particular class, and which reflect the basic economic interests of that class. For example, to maintain that slavery or serfdom is morally justifiable, or that profiting from the ownership of slaves or serfs is compatible with Christian morality, is to maintain views that are clearly in the interest of the class of slaveowners or hereditary lords, rather than in the interest of the slaves or serfs. Marxism does not hold that each class is right from its own viewpoint (if what is meant by this is that somehow all viewpoints can be taken as equally right).

Basically the Marxist argues, as we have seen, that there is a moral standard (derived from natural not supernatural sources) that should be recognized as binding upon all, and which can be broadly expressed as the welfare of all, the full, all-around growth and development of all. He further argues that at any particular period the struggles between the existing classes are of such a nature that the implementation of the class morality of some existing class brings society closer to the fulfillment of the standard that is best for all than the implementation of the class morality of some other existing class. For instance, the victory of capitalist principles over feudal principles was good for society, because it increased the possibilities of human development for more people. By the same standard, the victory of socialist principles over capitalist ones will also be good for society. The class interests of the proletariat or working class give it a more powerful motive than any other class has to champion the moral ideal of a classless society, and to work for the practical fulfillment of that ideal, because, while suffering heavy class oppression, it is closest to the practical means and methods necessary to the successful construction of socialism, i.e., to the elimination of classes. These means and methods must include familiarity with industrial technology, and political awareness and discipline. The peasantry is backward in these respects, though it also suffers heavy oppression.

8. *Does the Marxist approach to art constitute a sociology of art rather than a philosophy of art?*

It implies both. Marxism in general emphasizes the importance of the interrelationship of social factors with all aspects of philosophy, as we have seen. Philosophy of art cannot restrict itself to the consideration of esthetic forms (apart from content), or to esthetic experience as such (apart from the moral import of that experience), without an undue sacrifice of its own vitality and significance. Every work of art is an individual psychological source of esthetic emotions; but it is also much more than that. It is a molder of tastes and preferences, a protagonist of certain values; it creates sympathies and antipathies; intentionally or unintentionally, it promotes the acceptance (conscious or unconscious) of various forms of behavior, ways of life, types of social institution. In short, whether or not it so chooses, art is a teacher and a source of moral and social influence. For these reasons, the philosophy of art must be much more than purely esthetic analysis. It must seriously consider such questions as the purpose of art, the role of art in society, the relation of art to morality. The avoidance of questions of this kind by the philosopher of art usually amounts in practice to the attitude of "art for art's sake," which is one way of answering these questions, one thesis about the purpose, role, and moral status of art, but one that Marxism does not regard as either self-evident or well grounded. Moreover, it must be remembered that esthetic analysis as such is not confined to art, since beauty and the source of all other esthetic values are found in nature and life, apart from art.

9. *Is it possible to take a materialist or scientific approach to the analysis of beauty?*

It is, although such an approach is historically only in its beginning stages. Not only may the feeling of beauty (the emotions experienced by persons when they are in process of perceiving or appreciating what they consider to be beautiful) be analyzed psychologically in order to find basic, common factors at the level of subjective experience; it is also possible to seek and to find causative factors that are common to the wide variety of differing judgments about what is beautiful, and thus to arrive at rational explanations of this variety. A beginning along this line, often favorably mentioned by Soviet Marxists, is found in the work of the nineteenth-century Russian thinker—not a Marxist—N. G. Chernyshevsky, *The Aesthetic Relation of Art to Reality*.[3] He holds that observation and experience show that people call beautiful and feel to be beautiful that which suggests to them

life—life as they would like it to be. According to Chernyshevsky, there are different standards of beauty because the ideas of people about what they would like for
their lives are different; and these ideas are different because people live under different sets of conditions, have
different kinds of needs, and thus set up different ideals.
If one examines the difference that exists, for example,
between the ideals of personal beauty that are held by
the peasantry, on one side, and the nobility on the
other, as expressed in literature, songs, folk tales, and
events of daily life, one sees that the peasant associates
beauty with various characteristics that fit in with the
type of life he accepts as good and wishes to live, which
have a functional relation to the living of that kind of
life in fuller and happier measure—robustness, physical
strength, glowing health, and the like; however, such
characteristics are not necessary, or are even drawbacks,
in relation to the predominant standards of the nobles.
The latter make their judgments in terms of the kind of
life that conditions them, in terms of what fits in with
such a life, what makes it fuller and happier of its kind.
Thus the beautiful, in addition to being conceived in
functional terms, must also be conceived in social terms,
since man necessarily functions socially. To understand
the way in which beauty is felt and conceived, it must be
related to the living individual's needs (which, of course,
are not only physiological). This thesis is not contra-
dicted by the fact that people characterize a certain
painting of death or suffering as beautiful, for they associate the beauty not with the state of death or suffering,
but with the skill of the artist in depicting it, with the
effects such skill can create. That skill is a desirable

function of life; the beholder would like its powers and effects to be part of his own life.

10. *In what sense is romanticism considered to be compatible with social realism?*

In the sense, first of all, that there are in fact romantic aspects of life—that people do think, feel, and act in the ways generally designated by the term "romantic"—just as there are in fact romantic aspects of nature. The real includes the romantic, not only in this simple factual sense, but in the sense in which the real is a development, a movement and evolution into higher and more complex stages. Social reality is something that is evolving through the struggles and activities of people. It would be impossible to do justice to these struggles and activities without utilizing the qualities that are associated with romanticism, because a central part of their content is precisely the fighting of a battle to attain an ideal, the feeling of people that it is possible for them to make their lives better.

Notes

CHAPTER 2

1.   The thought underlying this law and the following (Excluded Middle) can be stated in many different ways, e.g., "The same thing, A, cannot both be and not be B," or "A cannot be both B and non-B." What is meant, of course, is *at the same time and in the same respect*. All will admit that the same thing (a pencil, for example) can be both black and non-black at the same time, in the sense that one part may be black and another part a different color. But Aristotle would say that such a pencil is not black and non-black *in the same respect*. To be simultaneously black and non-black in the same respect the very same black part would have to be simultaneously non-black. In his *Metaphysics* (1005^b, Ross trans.) Aristotle puts it this way: "It is, that the same attribute cannot at the same time belong and not belong to the same subject and in the same respect . . ."

2.   Frederick Engels, *Anti-Dühring* (*Herr Eugen Dühring's Revolution in Science*) (New York: International Publishers, 1939), p. 132.

CHAPTER 3

1.   Karl Marx, A *Contribution to the Critique of Political Economy*, quoted in John Somerville and Ronald E. Santoni, *Social and Political Philosophy* (Garden City, N. Y.: Doubleday, 1963), pp. 379–380.

2.   Karl Popper, *The Poverty of Historicism* (New York: Harper & Row, 1964), pp. vi–vii.

3.   *Ibid.*, p. vii.

CHAPTER 4

1. In his *The Class Struggles in France*, quoted in John Somerville, *Methodology in Social Science: A Critique of Marx and Engels* (New York: Lewin, 1938), p. 61.

2. See footnote 1, Chapter 3.

3. In his *The April Conference*, quoted in John Somerville, *The Communist Trials and the American Tradition* (New York: Cameron, 1956), p. 84.

4. In his *Marxism and Insurrection*, written about two months before the Bolshevik Revolution of November 7, 1917, and quoted in John Somerville, *The Communist Trials and the American Tradition* (New York: Cameron, 1956), pp. 75–76: "We have the following of the majority."

5. V. I. Lenin, *Selected Works*, Vol. VI (New York: International Publishers; Moscow: Foreign Languages Publishing House), p. 293.

6. See Benito Mussolini, *The Political and Social Doctrine of Fascism*, quoted in John Somerville and Ronald E. Santoni, *Social and Political Philosophy: Readings from Plato to Gandhi* (Garden City, N. Y.: Doubleday, 1963), p. 433.

7. See Adolf Hitler, *Mein Kampf*, quoted in John Somerville and Ronald E. Santoni, *op. cit.*, p. 458.

8. See G. M. Stekloff, *History of the First International*, (New York: International Publishers, 1928).

9. *Idem.*

10. *Program of the Communist Party of the Soviet Union, Adopted by the 22nd Congress of the C.P.S.U. October 31, 1961* (New York: Cross Currents Press, 1961), p. 70.

11. Quoted in John Somerville, *The Philosophy of Peace* (New York: Liberty, 1954), p. 28.

12. Adolf Hitler, *Mein Kampf* (New York: Reynal and Hitchcock, 1932), p. 175.

13. Benito Mussolini, *The Political and Social Doctrine of Fascism* (London: Hogarth Press, 1933).

14. See the article of P. N. Fedoseev (Vice President of the U.S.S.R. Academy of Sciences and Director of its Institute of Philosophy), "Contemporary Sociological Theories Concerning War and Peace," in *Soviet Studies in Philosophy, A Journal of Translation*, I, 3 (1962–1963), 3–25. See also his remarks in John Somerville and Dale Riepe, "The American-Soviet Philosophic Conference in Mexico," in the same journal, III, 2 (1964), 56–62.

15. Friedrich Engels, *Herr Eugen Dühring's Umwälzung der Wissenschaft* (Stuttgart: Dietz, 1904), p. 112.

16. See V. I. Lenin, *Materialism and Empirio-Criticism*, translated by Kvitko in *Collected Works of V. I. Lenin*, Vol. XIII (New York: International Publishers, 1927), p. 154.

17. Friedrich Engels, *Anti-Dühring*, translated by Emile Burns, (New York: International Publishers, 1935), p. 130.

18. Quoted in John Somerville, *Soviet Philosophy: A Study of Theory and Practice* (New York: Philosophical Library, 1946), p. 60.

19. Preface to the second edition of the first volume of his *Capital* (Chicago: Kerr, 1919).

CHAPTER 5

1. "We have shown what are the necessary conditions, and what are the parts of a state: husbandmen, craftsmen, and laborers of all kinds are necessary to the existence of states, but the parts of the state are the warriors and councillors." Aristotle, *Politics*, Book VII, 9, translated by Benjamin Jowett. In John Somerville and Ronald E. Santoni, *Social and Political Philosophy* (Garden City, N. Y.: Doubleday, 1963).

2. Cf. John Somerville, *Soviet Philosophy, A Study of Theory and Practice* (New York: Philosophical Library, 1946), Chapter IV.

3. Included in N. G. Chernyshevsky, *Selected Philosophical Essays* (Moscow: Foreign Languages Publishing House, 1953).

Index

STUDIES IN MARXISM

STUDIES IN MARXISM is a series of books providing discussions of important issues in all fields of knowledge from the dialectical-materialist perspective.

Conference proceedings volumes:

Vol. 1: **MARXISM AND NEW LEFT IDEOLOGY.** Proceedings of the First Midwest Marxist Scholars Conference, 1976. *Ed. by Ileana Rodríguez and William L. Rowe. 1977.*

Vol. 2: **SOCIAL CLASS IN THE CONTEMPORARY UNITED STATES.** Papers from the Second Midwest Marxist Scholars Conference, May 1977. *Ed. by Gerald M. Erickson and Harold L. Schwartz. 1977.*

Vol. 4: **THE UNITED STATES IN CRISIS: MARXIST ANALYSES.** Papers form the Third Midwest Marxist Scholars Conference, March 1978. *Ed. by Lajos Biro and Marc J. Cohen.* 1979.

Vol. 6: **THE UNITED STATES EDUCATIONAL SYSTEM: MARXIST APPROACHES.** Papers from the Fourth Midwest Marxist Scholars Conference, March 1979. *Ed. by Marvin J. Berlowitz and Frank E. Chapman, Jr.* 1980.

Volumes on special topics:

Vol. 3: **THE SOCIALIST COUNTRIES: GENERAL FEATURES OF POLITICAL, ECONOMIC, AND CULTURAL LIFE.** By Erwin Marquit. 1978.

Vol. 5: **NICARAGUA IN REVOLUTION: THE POETS SPEAK.** *Ed. by Bridget Aldaraca, Edward Baker, Ileana Rodríguez, and Marc Zimmerman.* Poems in Spanish, and in English translation, portraying long struggle against Somoza regime and imperialism. 1980.

Vol. 7: **PHILOSOPHICAL PROBLEMS IN PHYSICAL SCIENCE.** *By Herbert Hörz, Hans-Dieter Pöltz, Heinrich Parthey, Ulrich Röseberg, and Karl-Friedrich Wessel.* First publication in English of outstanding text from the German Democratic Republic. 1980.

Vol. 8: **PROGRESSIVE EDUCATION: A MARXIST INTERPRETATION.** *By Gilbert G. Gonzalez.* Includes special section on harmful consequences of application of Dewey's theories to Chicano community in Los Angeles. 1981.

Vol. 9: **THE PHILOSOPHY OF MARXISM: AN EXPOSITION.** *By John Somerville.* Well-known introductory text again available. Unmatched excellence for classroom use. Popular style. Reprint of 1967 edition. 1981.

Vol. 10: **DIALECTICAL CONTRADICTIONS.** *Ed. by Erwin Marquit, Philip Moran, and Willis H. Truitt.* Unique international collection deals with the theory of dialectical contradictions and its applications in various fields. 1981.

Vol. 11: **DEATH RATTLES: CRISIS-CONSCIOUSNESS PHILOSOPHY IN BOURGEOIS SOCIETY.** *By András Gedő.* Penetrating analysis by outstanding Hungarian philosopher. 1981.

Order from: MARXIST EDUCATIONAL PRESS, c/o Anthropology Department, 215 Ford Hall, University of Minnesota, 224 Church Street S.E., Minneapolis, Minnesota 55455.